THE PRINCETON REVIEW

LSAT GRE Analytic workout

Cracking the ACT
Cracking the ACT with Sample Tests on CD-ROM
Cracking the CLEP (College-Level Examination Program)
Cracking the GED
Cracking the GMAT
Cracking the GMAT with Sample Tests on Computer Disk
Cracking the GRE
Cracking the GRE with Sample Tests on Computer Disk
Cracking the GRE Biology Subject Test
Cracking the GRE Literature in English Subject Test
Cracking the GRE Psychology Subject Test
Cracking the LSAT
Cracking the LSAT with Sample Tests on Computer Disk
Cracking the LSAT with Sample Tests on CD-ROM
Cracking the MAT (Miller Analogies Test)
Cracking the SAT and PSAT
Cracking the SAT and PSAT with Sample Tests on Computer Disk
Cracking the SAT and PSAT with Sample Tests on CD-ROM
Cracking the SAT II: Biology Subject Test
Cracking the SAT II: Chemistry Subject Test
Cracking the SAT II: English Subject Tests
Cracking the SAT II: French Subject Test
Cracking the SAT II: History Subject Tests
Cracking the SAT II: Math Subject Tests
Cracking the SAT II: Physics Subject Test
Cracking the SAT II: Spanish Subject Test
Cracking the TOEFL with Audiocassette
Flowers & Silver MCAT
Flowers Annotated MCAT
Flowers Annotated MCATs with Sample Tests on Computer Disk
Flowers Annotated MCATs with Sample Tests on CD-ROM

Culturescope Grade School Edition
Culturescope High School Edition
Culturescope College Edition

SAT Math Workout
SAT Verbal Workout

All U Can Eat
Don't Be a Chump!
How to Survive Without Your Parents' Money
Speak Now!
Trashproof Resumes

Biology Smart
Grammar Smart
Math Smart
Reading Smart
Study Smart
Word Smart: Building an Educated Vocabulary
Word Smart II: How to Build a More Educated Vocabulary
Word Smart Executive
Word Smart Genius
Writing Smart

Grammar Smart Junior
Math Smart Junior
Word Smart Junior
Writing Smart Junior

Business School Companion
College Companion
Law School Companion
Medical School Companion

Student Access Guide to College Admissions
Student Advantage Guide to the Best 310 Colleges
Student Advantage Guide to America's Top Internships
Student Advantage Guide to Business Schools
Student Advantage Guide to Law Schools
Student Advantage Guide to Medical Schools
Student Advantage Guide to Paying for College
Student Advantage Guide to Summer
Student Advantage Guide to Visiting College Campuses
Student Advantage Guide: Help Yourself
Student Advantage Guide: The Complete Book of Colleges
Student Advantage Guide: The Internship Bible
Hillel Guide to Jewish Life on Campus
International Students' Guide to the United States
The Princeton Review Guide to Your Career

Also available on cassette from Living Language
Grammar Smart
Word Smart
Word Smart II

THE PRINCETON REVIEW

LSAT GRE Analytic
Workout

By Karen Lurie

Random House, Inc.
New York 1996
http://www.randomhouse.com

Princeton Review Publishing, L.L.C.
2315 Broadway, 3rd Floor
New York, NY 10024
e-mail: info@review.com

Library of Congress Cataloging-in-Publication Data

Lurie, Karen, 1965-

   The Princeton Review LSAT/GRE Analytic Workout / by Karen Lurie.
   p.   cm.

   ISBN: 0-679-77358-4

   1. Graduate Record Examination--Study guides.   2. Law School
Admissions Test--Study guides. 3. Logic.   4. Reasoning.
I. Princeton Review (Firm)   II. Title.
LB2367 .4.L87   1996
378.1'662--dc20   96-21088
                                                                CIP

Edited by Celeste Sollod and Kristin Fayne-Mulroy.

Designed by Meher Khambata.

Manufactured in the United States of America on partially recycled paper.

9 8 7 6 5 4 3 2 1

First Edition

ACKNOWLEDGMENTS

The author would like to thank the following people for their help: Andy Dunn, Heather Elliot, Kristin Fayne-Mulroy, John Flansburgh, Nell Goddin, Chris Kensler, John Linnell, Andy Lutz, Ken Riley, Rick Rodstrom, Dave Schaller, Celeste Sollod, and Jeannie Yoon. And thanks to John Bergdahl, Greta Englert, Effie Hadjiioannou, Sung(Peter) Jung, Meher Khambata, Illeny Maaza, Chun(John) Pak, and Matthew Reilly for the art, layout and design of this book.

TABLE OF CONTENTS

CHAPTER 1

Orientation

READ THIS STUFF FIRST

You may know them as "Analytical Reasoning." You may refer to them as "Logic Games." Or, you may call them hellish. But we call them games, and you want to learn how to improve on them. If you're taking the LSAT, you are facing a whole section of them, which is about one-fourth of your test. If you're taking the GRE, you're facing one (for the CAT) or two (for the paper-and-pencil) sections that include them.

This book will tell you everything you ever wanted to know about games, starting with this piece of comforting news—games just happen to be one of the easiest test question types to improve on. The Princeton Review, an international test prep company, gives courses which I have been teaching for many years, and these courses have been very successful in improving people's ability to do games.

HOW TO USE THIS BOOK

Besides this book, you should also get a hold of some real LSATs or GREs. Take the games section of the most recent LSAT you can find (in timed, test-like conditions), or take a timed Analytic Section from a recent GRE. This way, you expose yourself as soon as possible to the experience, and the pacing tips in this book will already make more sense to you.

After you take your first real section, use this book to learn all the techniques for improving on games. Once you learn the techniques, the most effective way to improve on games is to practice games. That's why so much of this book is made up of the games themselves. This way you can immerse yourself in them. When you've sufficiently "worked out," you'll be ready to take more real, timed test sections and gauge your improvement.

But in order to improve your score, you first need to know just what games are.

WHAT IS A GAME?

A game is nothing more than a set of rules that allows for a limited number of variations in the way a set of elements can be arranged. It's kind of like solitaire. You organize and manipulate the elements according to these rules, NOT by using mathematical or verbal logic.

If, during a given week, you wanted to see a movie on a weeknight, and you knew you had to work Monday, Wednesday, and Friday nights, what could you conclude? That you should go see the movie either on Tuesday or Thursday night. Congratulations! You just made the kind of deduction that games are based on.

A game presents elements that have some kind of relationship. The initial information describes that relationship and its elements. We call the initial information the *setup*. How these elements can and cannot relate to each other is described in a series of conditions or requirements. We call these conditions *clues*. The clues give you only partial information about the game. The questions themselves often provide additional clues that may be used only for that question.

Here's a sample so you can see the anatomy of a game. Don't write anything down—you'll get a chance to do this one later. The first paragraph is the setup, and the indented sentences are the clues:

Shelf
Letter ⎤ *— 3 conditions*
Color ⎦

set up {

In a window display, there are five teapots, A, B, C, D, and E. Each teapot is a different color: red, orange, yellow, green, or blue. The display has two shelves, a left shelf and a right shelf; three teapots are displayed on the left shelf, the other two on the right shelf. The display must meet the following additional conditions:

clues {

A is displayed on the right shelf.
B is displayed on the left shelf and is not orange.
C is not displayed on a shelf where the green teapot is displayed.
E is the yellow teapot.
The orange teapot and the yellow teapot are displayed on the same shelf.

— — — | — —

B - not O

(A)

C - not w/ green

Here are two questions that might follow this game:

1. If C is displayed on the left shelf, which one of the following must be true?

   (A) The yellow teapot is displayed on the right shelf.
   (B) The orange teapot is displayed on the right shelf.
   (C) D is displayed on the right shelf.
   (D) D is displayed on the left shelf.
   (E) The green teapot is displayed on the left shelf.

2. Which one of the following must be true?

   (A) The yellow teapot is on the right shelf.
   (B) The red teapot is on the left shelf.
   (C) The orange teapot is on the right shelf.
   (D) The orange teapot is on the left shelf.
   (E) The green teapot is on the right shelf.

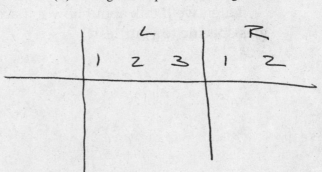

WHERE ARE THEY?

On the LSAT, games have their own section. The Games Section contains four games, with 5-8 questions each, for a total of 24 questions. The test writers allow you 35 minutes to answer these questions.

On the paper-and-pencil GRE, the section on which you will see games is called the Analytic Section, but it also contains what we call (and will not discuss in this book) Arguments, which are those little paragraphs followed by a question or two. Don't worry, you won't mistake them for games. There are 3 or 4 games per section (totaling 16-19 questions). You'll have 30 minutes for the Analytic Section, including games and arguments.

On the computer-adaptive GRE (GRE CAT), there are 35 questions (including both games and arguments) in the Analytic Section. The Analytic Section on the GRE CAT includes roughly 4-7 games with two to five questions each; roughly 20-25 questions on this section will be with games. You have 60 minutes for the entire section.

TEST	HOW MANY GAMES	TOTAL TIME
LSAT	4 games with roughly 5-8 questions each; 24 questions total	35 minutes
GRE paper-and-pencil	3-4 games with roughly 4-7 questions each; 16-19 questions total	30 minutes (this section includes other question types)
GRE CAT	4-7 games with roughly 2 to 5 questions each; 20-25 questions total	60 minutes (this section includes other question types)

Later, we'll talk about how to pace yourself and how to employ strategies specific to your test.

NO EXPERIENCE REQUIRED

You never had to do anything like this before you saw your first LSAT or GRE, and this is not covered in any college course. But say you were planning the seating arrangement for your sister's wedding, and your Aunt Selma and your grandmother haven't spoken since 1958, so they can't be seated at the same table and... well, you get the idea. And that's really what you're doing when you're doing a game—organizing information within guidelines.

Doing games is something you must learn, not something to rummage around in your brain and remember, like math. This is good news because you haven't had time to talk yourself into "not being able" to do them; we're starting from scratch. (It's so cleansing, isn't it?) You must always remember that, as with any standardized test like the GRE or the LSAT, your intelligence is not being tested. Your ability to do games is not directly, or even indirectly, connected to how smart you are. Standardized tests only measure how well you do on standardized tests.

Let's delve a little deeper. You might not learn to love games so much that you want to wake up every morning and do them instead of the crossword puzzle, but you might find that they aren't the ordeal that you thought they were. It's even possible that you'll come to find that games are the fun part, relative to the rest of the material on your test.

CHAPTER

2

Strategies

THE DIRECTIONS

Here are the directions for the Analytic Section (the one containing games) on the GRE:

Directions: Each question or group of questions is based on a passage, graph, table, or set of conditions. In answering some of the questions, it may be useful to draw a rough diagram. For each question, select the best answer choice given.

Here are the LSAT Games Section directions:

Directions: Each group of questions in this section is based on a set of conditions. In answering some of the questions, it may be useful to draw a rough diagram. Choose the response that most accurately and completely answers each question and blacken the corresponding space on your answer sheet.

Pretty similar, huh? My favorite part is "it may be useful to draw a rough diagram." May be?

> Using diagrams and symbols is the only way to solve games.

Thanks

Keep that in mind, and you never have to read these directions again.

WHAT WAS THAT ABOUT DIAGRAMS?

You should never, ever rely on your memory when doing games. You have to write everything down, on your test booklet if you're taking the LSAT or paper-and-pencil GRE, or on your scrap paper if you're taking the GRE CAT. You don't have to be an artist, though. You'll learn all about what you have to do as you read this book. Just remember: from now on, don't do ANYTHING in your head. Don't even think about it.

THE PROCESS

Here's some good news: no matter which test you're taking, in the world of games, there are two types: Assignment and Non-assignment. And here's some more good news: there is only one process that you need to follow to figure out any game.

Step 1: Decide on the appropriate diagram and draw it.

Step 2: Symbolize the clues.

Step 3: Double-check your work and make deductions.

Step 4: Decide question order (not for GRE CAT).

Step 5: Keep your pencil moving.

You'll be seeing these steps again and again. Memorize them. They will make more sense when you see them in action, and they will crack every game every time. They are your ticket to more points on the LSAT and GRE.

NO GUESSING PENALTY

> There is no penalty for guessing on the LSAT or the GRE.

If you're taking the GRE CAT, you have no choice but to mark an answer to whatever question is on the screen. You can't move on without doing so. If you're taking the paper-and-pencil GRE or the LSAT, you should NEVER leave anything blank on your answer sheet. Ever. So, if while reading this book, you see references to skipping questions or whole games, be perfectly straight on this point: that doesn't mean to leave it blank on your answer sheet. That just means don't do any work on the game or the question. Repeat after me: "I will not leave blanks."

PRACTICE

Why does over half of this book consist of sample games? Because practice is everything. There is no theory to embrace, no philosophy to comprehend, no details to cram the night before. You must concentrate on following our consistent procedure. Use our outline of the techniques, and have it in front of you as you practice games.

If you are taking the LSAT or the paper and pencil GRE, do your work in the book; don't use scrap paper. You don't get to use it on the test, so don't get used to using it in practice.

If you are taking the GRE CAT, you should use the scrap paper included in the back of this book, since you get to use it for your test. You might even want to practice these games by standing this book up, as if you were reading a computer screen, since that's what it will be like when you take your exam.

Here are some tips on practicing games:

- Do everything in pencil, and don't erase your work.

- If a particular symbol (you'll learn about them soon) isn't helping, or is even causing mistakes, stop using it. Try something else.

- Only practice games when you are able to give them your full attention. You have to be really careful when you do them. A game is a test of how careful you can be. If you're distracted while doing one, you'll make mistakes, and you'll think it's because you "can't do them." You CAN do them, if you concentrate.

SPACE MANAGEMENT

How you use the space you're given is a very important consideration when you're doing games. Remember, if you are taking the LSAT or the paper-and-pencil GRE, you will not get any scrap paper. At all. Period. So you must learn to draw your diagrams in the space provided, which isn't much. A good way to practice cramming diagrams into a small space is to get a normal-sized pad of sticky notes (the 2 1/2 inch by 2 1/2 inch size). If you can fit your whole diagram and all of your symbols onto one sticky note, you're doing fine.

Those of you taking the GRE CAT don't have to worry your pretty little heads about space management. You get scrap paper! Use the scrap paper in the back of this book when practicing the games.

DON'T RUSH

When doing games, keep telling yourself "accuracy, not speed." You don't have to finish every question in a section. Your goal is to get what you do work on correct. For every person reading this book, that means slowing down and being extra careful.

IF YOU'RE TAKING THE LSAT

Your special task as an LSAT-taker is ordering the Games Section. As you now know, the Games Section contains four games, with 5-8 questions each, for a total of 24 questions in 35 minutes. You earn no partial credit and no extra points for "finishing" the section. In fact, finishing the section can, and probably will, hurt your score. Remember, the goal is accuracy, not speed. Your score is based on the number of questions that you answer correctly, not on how many you attempt. Do fewer questions, and get them right. Rushing through all 24 questions and only getting twelve right isn't any better than slowing down, only doing two games in those 35 minutes, and getting all twelve questions you do right. So if you commit to a game, get every question right. Then, with practice you can work on increasing your speed, do three games instead of two, and get all of those questions right. Then you'd be getting 75 percent correct instead of rushing and only getting half correct. That's how it works. (Of course you know that "skipping" a game means not looking at it, but still filling in the bubbles on your answer sheet.)

Make sure you know how many games you are supposed to do. Roughly, if you get 50 percent or fewer correct answers on a games section (take a practice section timed from a real LSAT and find out!), do only two games the next time you take one; if you get between 50 and 75 percent, do three next time; if you get above 75 percent, do all four next time. Fifty percent is twelve questions right out of 24; 75 percent is 18. You cannot go from 50 percent to 100 percent in one shot. You must build toward your ultimate goal. If you are at 50 percent, you first have to get to 75 percent. Then you can get to 100 percent.

The questions on the LSAT are not arranged in order of difficulty; in other words, the questions don't start out easy and get harder, as they do on the GRE. So, you have to pick the right games, and do them in the right order. The first thing you do when you get to the Games Section is order the section. That means you take the first minute or two to read the four setups and rank them in order from easy to hard. That is the order in which you do them. Ordering the section is a crucial step no matter how many games you plan to do during the test; doing the easier ones first will get you warmed up for the harder ones. Also, if you run out of time, you will already have done the ones you were most likely to get right and skipped the ones you were most likely to miss.

When you are ordering the games section, here are some things to consider:

- **Is it an Assignment Game?** Generally, Assignment Games are easier than other types. You'll learn how to recognize them later.

- **Do you know what diagram to use?** If you don't know how to diagram it, skip it. You should be able to see the diagram forming in your head as you read the setup. You'll learn more about this later, too.

- **Do you know EXACTLY how many elements are going in how many places?** Do you have one element for each space on your diagram? Good. Do you have four elements being assigned to five slots, and any element can be assigned more than once, or not at all? Not as good.

- **How "good" are the clues?** You want the elements to be as restricted as possible, because restrictions limit the number of possible variations. "N always leaves last" is a good clue. "Mike arrives immediately after Joel" is a good clue. "There are no more than four trumpet players in each of the bands" is not a good clue.

- **What are the questions like?** The games with more "If" questions are usually easier.

Nothing will mess you up more than doing the games in the wrong order. You need to know how to recognize the easier games so you can do them first. Seventy-five to one hundred percent of the games on the LSAT are Assignment, so make sure you know those cold.

Come back to this page after you've practiced a few games, when these tips will make more sense to you.

IF YOU'RE TAKING THE PAPER-AND-PENCIL GRE

The games on the paper-and-pencil GRE are arranged in order of difficulty for you. This is good news. You don't have to worry about diagnosing whether the game is easy or hard. There are 3 or 4 games per section (totaling 16-19 questions). The section on which you will see games is called the Analytic Section, and it also contains Arguments, those little paragraphs followed by a question or two. Because this section is ordered from easy to hard, all you really need to think about is pacing yourself. To get the best score on this section, you should focus on answering the easy questions, then the medium questions. Don't push yourself to finish the section, because your score is based on the number of questions that you answer correctly, not on how many you attempt.

You can get a 600 on the Analytic Section of the paper and pencil GRE by only answering questions 1 through 16 (and, of course, filling something in for 17 through 25, because there's no guessing penalty). This means that if 600, or even 650, is your goal, you might never even have to look at the hardest (last) game in the section. That's pretty good news. But that means you have to be accurate in your responses to the easy and medium games questions, which means slowing down and being careful. In a way, games are a test of how well you read. If you miss the word "only" or the word "exactly" in a clue, you'll screw up the game.

This chart will give you an idea of how to pace yourself on the paper and pencil GRE:

Score	Work Out Correctly	Fill in Bubbles For
400	questions 1- 8	9-25
450	questions 1-10	11-25
500	questions 1-12	13-25
550	questions 1-14	15-25
600	questions 1-16	17-25
650	questions 1-18	19-25
700	questions 1-20	21-25
750	questions 1-23	24-25
800	questions 1-24	25

IF YOU'RE TAKING THE COMPUTER-ADAPTIVE GRE (GRE CAT)

You've got two things in your favor. You get scrap paper, and (relatively) lots of time. You have 60 minutes for the Analytic Section on the computer-adaptive GRE. There are 35 questions, including both games and arguments. Roughly 20-25 questions on this section will be games, which works out to 4–7 games.

On the CAT, you must be sure that you are picking what you feel is the right answer. You cannot go back to check your work once you pick an answer, and you cannot skip any question to come back to it later. You should be extra careful on the first few questions in the section, because these first few questions go a long way toward determining your score. Why? Because the computer is "adapting" after each question to try to "find your score." If you get the first few questions, you're starting out on better ground and can keep building. If you keep missing the early ones, it takes longer to bring your score back up.

The key to doing well on the games on the GRE CAT, just like on every other part of the GRE CAT, is your use of scrap paper. You must be extra careful in creating your diagram and symbols on scrap paper, because you have to be able to read the screen and refer to you notes, and both have to make sense. Don't ever be afraid to write stuff down—you can never write down too much.

Feel free to refer back to this pacing information after you've read the other chapters in the book and understand the process a little better. Now, are you ready to get into the true grit of games? Then turn the page.

3

Nuts and Bolts

HERE IT IS AGAIN, THE STEP-BY-STEP GAMES PROCESS:

Step 1: Decide on the appropriate diagram and draw it.

Step 2: Symbolize the clues.

Step 3: Double-check your work and make deductions.

Step 4: Decide question order (not for GRE CAT).

Step 5: Keep your pencil moving.

But what does it really mean?

STEP 1: DECIDE ON THE APPROPRIATE DIAGRAM AND DRAW IT

For this first step, you need to be able to see the diagram forming in your mind as you read the setup and clues. You can't do Step 1 unless you know which diagrams work on which game types.

ASSIGNMENT GAMES

No matter which test you are preparing for, the majority of the games you will see will be Assignment Games. That's guaranteed. In an Assignment Game, you're asked to assign things to places. The places might be ages, or cars, or shelves, or classrooms, or boats, or seats in a theater. The things you're assigning could be people, toasters, hot dogs, diseases, or colors. It's as if you actually had on the desk in front of you three cars and nine people to arrange in the cars in various combinations.

What's on Top

The way to solve an Assignment Game, in most cases, is to make some kind of grid. A grid looks like this:

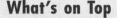

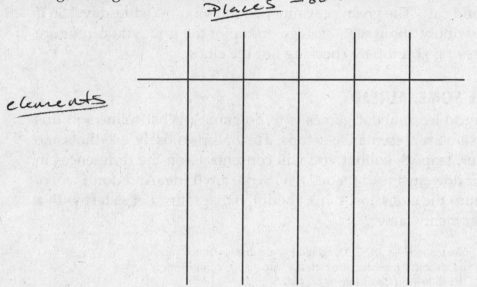

Places — do not △

elements

The things you are assigning, called the elements, are listed somewhere to the left of the grid, (or wherever you have room), and the places you're assigning the elements to go on top of the grid.

How do you know what goes on top of the diagram? Often, things with a natural order, such as rooms numbered 1 through 4, days of the week, or hours of the day, will be lined up on the top of your grid. But what if the game isn't about days of the week or things lined up in a consecutive order? Don't worry—you always put what *doesn't change* on top of the diagram. For example: Nine people ride to work each day in three cars. The three cars don't change, but who rides with whom will change, depending on the question. So, you put the cars on top and the people underneath, in varying combinations according to the questions.

In order to figure out what goes on top of your grid, don't just read the opening paragraph, or setup. And don't just slap numbers down on the top of the grid. You should *read the clues* as well. Sometimes you won't know what to do, or won't see the diagram forming in your mind's eye until you read the clues. Reading the clues clears everything up. Here's why: the clues are always about the elements, not the places. The clues are always about the things that move, the things that change. For example, you would never see a clue that says "Wednesday cannot be shown on the green car." The clue would say "The green car cannot be shown on Wednesday." So if you're in any doubt about what *does* go on top of the grid, you can figure out what *doesn't* go on top by checking out the clues.

SO LET'S SEE SOME, ALREADY

The best way to learn about games is to do games. What follows in this chapter are some representative setups. They all purposely use the same subject matter, teapots, so that you will concentrate on the differences in structure. For now, just read them. Don't write anything. And don't worry too much about the clues; just think about the diagrams. Let's start with a typical Assignment Game:

> Six teapots—A, B, C, D, E, and F—are displayed in a row on a shelf. The order in which they are displayed must meet the following conditions:
> F cannot be displayed next to C.
> E cannot be displayed next to D.
> D must be displayed next to A.

We have six teapots in a row, and clues about their order. What would you put on top? How about this:

1	2	3	4	5	6

Here's another one:

> Eight teapots—A, B, C, D, E, F, G, and H—are being
> displayed on three shelves. One of the shelves will hold
> two teapots, and the other two shelves will hold three
> teapots. The following conditions must be met:
>   B will be displayed on the two-teapot shelf.
>   C will not be displayed on the two-teapot shelf.
>   G shares a shelf with A.
>   H will not share a shelf with A.

This time, there are eight teapots and three shelves. Those shelves never change, but the combinations of teapots do. What would you put on top this time? How about this:

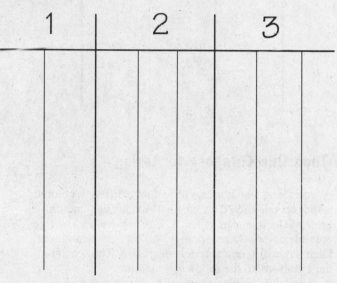

ASSIGNMENT VARIATIONS

There are variations on the Assignment theme, but these variations are still Assignment Games.

Not Every Element Gets Assigned

> Four teapots are being selected for a special window
> display. There are eight teapots to choose from—A, B, C,
> D, E, F, G, and H. The selection must be made according
> to the following conditions:
>   A cannot be selected unless B is also selected.
>   The display must include D or E or both.
>   The display cannot include both F and C.

We have to choose four teapots out of a possible eight. We're still assigning things to places, but the difference here is that not every element gets assigned. We need a place to put the elements that don't get assigned, the ones that are "out," so:

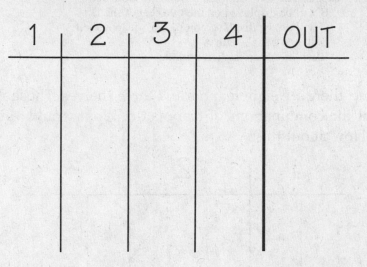

There's More Than One Category to Assign

A week-long teapot sale will feature a different colored teapot on sale each day, starting Monday and ending Friday. The five teapots are A, B, C, D, and E. The five possible colors are red, orange, yellow, green, and blue. Each day a different teapot is displayed. The schedule must conform to the following conditions:

    D can only be displayed on Wednesday or Friday.

    The orange teapot must be displayed on either the day immediately before or the day immediately after the day on which B is displayed.

    A and C must be displayed on consecutive days.

    E is not the red teapot.

    The yellow teapot must be displayed earlier in the week than the green teapot.

This time we have two "categories" of things to assign—teapots and colors. What could you do about that?

How about this:

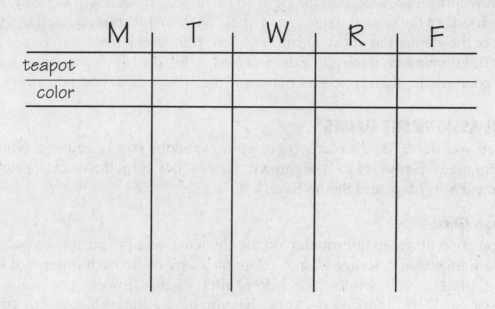

	M	T	W	R	F
teapot					
color					

Assigning Elements in a Shape

Six teapots are to be displayed in a circular window
display. The six teapots are A, B, C, D, E, and F. They
are to be equally spaced around the circular display
according to the following rules:
A must be placed next to F.
There is to be exactly one teapot between B and C.
C cannot be placed next to F.
D cannot be placed next to both A and C.

In this game, you're still assigning things to places, but this time the places weren't in a straight line. No problem. All you would do is draw the shape they tell you to draw.

Don't just draw a circle if that's the shape the game requires. First, they are hard to really draw accurately. Second, unless you are a really good artist, it will be hard for you to really show who is across from whom. Instead, draw an asterisk, with enough spaces for all the elements, like this:

This way, you can clearly see who is next to whom and who is across from whom. Also, who's on the right and who's on the left will depend on which side of the table the element in question is on. Just put yourself in the seat of the element in question, and use your right and left sides to figure it out. But remember, if the game doesn't make a big deal about the *exact* seat someone sits in, then it doesn't matter. If they don't care, you don't care.

NON-ASSIGNMENT GAMES

When you don't have a place to put your elements, you've found a Non-Assignment Game. Non-Assignment Games fall into three categories: Range, Path/Map, and Simon Says.

Range Games

If you are only given information on the elements' relative position, you've got a Range Game. Range Games relate the elements to each other, not to fixed places, with words like before/after, higher/lower, and faster/slower. So, Step 1 involves deciding that you have a Range Game, but you can't actually draw the diagram until you symbolize the clues. So, you complete Step 2 (Symbolize the clues). Then, on Step 3, when you are linking the clues, you create your flexible Range diagram. For example:

> The sales of six teapots—A, B, C, D, E, and F—are being
> compared. The following information is known about the
> relative sales of the teapots:
> A is a better seller than D, but is a worse seller than F.
> E is a better seller than C, but is a worse seller than A.
> B is not a better seller than F.

See? There's no place to put these teapots on a grid; we can only relate them *to each other*. You need a different kind of diagram for a Range Game. You'll see it later in this chapter, after you learn about clues and deductions, since this diagram is drawn after the clues are symbolized.

Path/Map Games

If your task when doing a game is to *connect* things, not assign things, you've found a Path/Map Game. Like in Range Games, Step 1 is more of a diagnosis, because you can't really draw the diagram until, after you've symbolized the clues (so you'll see this later). These games come in two flavors—either the elements are fixed and you have to make connections (in which case you should not have to redraw your diagram), or the elements are not fixed and you might have to redraw your diagram depending on the information in the question.

For example:

> Seven antique teapots—A, B, C, D, E, F, and G—are
> being displayed in a museum, and viewers must follow
> pathways to view all of the teapots. The route may only be
> entered and exited through a door located next to A. The
> following list includes all of the pathways:
>> There is a pathway connecting A to B, C, and E.
>> There is a pathway connecting B and C.
>> There is a pathway connecting E to D and to F.
>> There is a pathway connecting F and G.

See? Nothing to assign here. It's all about connections. You just draw it any way that makes sense to you. On the LSAT, these games are more likely to be about paths between things, like bridges connecting islands. On the GRE, they tend to be more like maps, like stops on a bus route, or memos being passed around by employees.

Simon Says

If all you can do in a game is follow directions, and switch, move, or mix things, you've got a Simon Says Game. We call these Simon Says Games because all you can do is sit back and take orders. Often these "orders" consist of a few different ways to change the order of things. For example:

> Teapots A, B, C and D are the only teapots involved in a
> water-boiling contest. In each round of the contest,
> different teas are being made, and the teapots are being
> judged on the speed with which they boil water. A teapot
> is eliminated the first time it fails to boil water fast
> enough. The teapots will be rearranged between rounds
> according to one of the following rules:
>> Darjeeling Rule: The teapot that was in third place
>> moves in front of the teapot that was previously in
>> first place.
>> Earl Grey Rule: The teapot that was in last place moves
>> into the first place position.
>> Orange Pekoe Rule: The teapot that was in third place
>> moves in front of the teapot that was previously in
>> second place.
>> If a rearrangement involves a place where a teapot has
>> been eliminated, that rearrangement cannot occur.
>> If none of the rearrangements can occur, the teapots
>> will remain in the same order as they were in the
>> preceding round.

- "Assignment"
- "Map"
- "Range"
- "Simon Says"

Whew! Nothing to assign here. All you can do is write down the initial setup, and wait for the questions to give you the information you need to switch and move these pots around.

Don't worry—you'll get a chance to see how the setups for all of these games look. You'll even get a chance to try them yourself. But first, on to...

STEP 2: SYMBOLIZE THE CLUES

The key to good symbols is making sure those symbols are consistent with your diagram. Avoid using words—the idea is to translate the words of the clue into something visual. Never rely on your memory for anything.

The most important, and common, clues you will need to know cold are *blocks* and *if-then clues*. Let's talk about blocks first.

BLOCKS

Blocks occur when one element is immediately above, below, to the right of, or to the left of, another element. Blocks restrict positions. The opposite of a block is an *antiblock*. That's when one element is NOT immediately above, below, to the right of, or to the left of, another element. Antiblocks also restrict positions. And restricting positions is the name of the game. You can't have blocks referring to what goes on top of your diagram, so blocks also help you figure out what goes on top and what doesn't (what doesn't will be your elements). We love blocks because they take up space on the diagram, limiting positions for the rest of the elements. Here are some examples of clues representing blocks and antiblocks, followed by the appropriate symbols:

The maple tree is next to the elm tree.

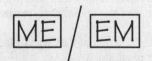

Notice the box around the elements. That's why it's called a block. These trees travel together. They're inseparable. Notice also that the clue does not indicate whether M is to the left or right of E. You must symbolize the block in both directions. If you don't, when you're doing the game, you might think M can only be on the left, and you'll be wrong. If you saw a clue that said "The pink hat and the blue hat are on the same shelf," it would still be a block, but it's not necessary to symbolize it in both directions. Why? Because the order of the hats doesn't matter. They are just together on the shelf.

The two plumbers never sit next to each other.

Notice the slash through the box. That's why it's called an antiblock.

Only Q stands between D and W.

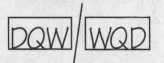

Notice this is going in both directions again. This is crucial!

The green car must be shown the day immediately after
the day on which the blue car is shown.

BG *Order no matter – just permutations*

Because this clue gives an order, the block should only go in the order given.

P cannot live on a floor immediately above or
immediately below the floor Q lives on.

Don't panic just because it's vertical. It's the same deal, but since your diagram will be vertical to reflect the floors of a building, your clues should be vertical too.

The pink vase is displayed immediately above the silver
vase.

Note that this clue does not go in both directions.

Those are standard block and antiblock clues. You saw lots of words like "next to" and "immediately," didn't you? Now, here are some variations on the block theme:

There are exactly two desks between Maria's desk and
Ruby's desk.

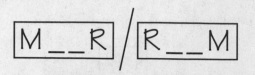

This is still a block. It just has some unknowns in there. It still takes up space.

Kelly lives two floors above Chauncey.

No, your eyes are not deceiving you. "Two floors above" means "one floor between." Think about it.

The stapler must be placed in a drawer in which only one other item is placed.

$$\boxed{S\_}$$

Perm.

Not only do blocks take up space and restrict positions, they're great for deductions, as you'll see later in this chapter.

IF-THEN CLUES

If-then clues are about conditions. They start with the word "If" most of the time. If the clue starts with "If," you symbolize it like this:

If Homer is chosen, then Marge is chosen.

$$H \longrightarrow M$$

That arrow is <u>not</u> an equal sign. It cannot be reversed. What this clue means is that Homer has a problem. Homer can't be chosen unless something happens. That something is Marge being chosen. However, Marge is free; she can be chosen or not be chosen. There is no *condition* on Marge, as there is on Homer.

Sometimes these standardized tests are not kind enough to start these clues with the word "If." They might start with "only" or "unless." *If* that's the case, *then* it's your job to figure out who has the problem. Whoever has the problem goes on the left side of the arrow. For example, what if the clue said:

Homer cannot be chosen unless Marge is chosen.

Who's got the problem? Who isn't free? Who can't do something unless something else happens? It's Homer. So the symbol is:

$$H \longrightarrow M$$

What if the clue said:

> Unless Marge is chosen, Homer cannot be chosen.

Who's got the problem? Who isn't free? Who can't do something unless something else happens? It's still Homer. So the symbol is still:

$$H \longrightarrow M$$

What if the clue said:

> Only if Marge is chosen will Homer be chosen.

Who's got the problem? Who isn't free? Who can't do something unless something else happens? Yes, it's still Homer. So the symbol is still:

$$H \longrightarrow M$$

Here are a bunch of conditional clues and their symbols. Cover up the symbols and try them yourself first, then uncover the symbols to check yourself:

> Unless Felicia is chosen, Julia cannot be chosen.

$$J \longrightarrow F$$

> If Liza is at the meeting, Ned cannot be at the meeting.

The little wavy line in front of the N means "not."

> If C is scheduled to work, then neither F nor H can be scheduled to work.

$$C \longrightarrow {\sim}F$$
$$C \longrightarrow {\sim}H$$

You must separate this into two clues, otherwise your symbol might be wrong. You can never be too careful.

If either mushrooms or onions is served, then both must
be served.

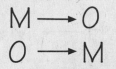

Is anyone out there thinking that this looks like a block? Well, you're right. But we'll get to that when we discuss deductions.

Only if Angie is chosen will Patrick be chosen.

If the train reaches all five stations, it must have gone
first to the blue station.

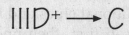

If three irises and at least one daffodil are chosen, the
chrysanthemum must also be chosen.

$$IIID^+ \longrightarrow C$$

What's that plus sign doing there? It means "at least."
We'll revisit these clues when we discuss deductions.

RANGE CLUES

Range clues don't only show up in Range Games. They show up in Assignment Games too. Range clues are about the relative order of the elements. Range clues are great for putting restrictions on your diagram in assignment games. They look like this:

Not as restrictive!

Todd left before Laura.

$$T . . . L$$

See, this isn't a block, because it doesn't say "Todd left IMMEDIATELY before Laura." The three dots mean "sometime."

Kevin scored more points than Tess.

$$K . . . T$$

Anita and Luke were hired before Mason.

$$A . . . M$$

$$L . . . M$$

Better separate these clues, just to be safe.

For those last two examples, you might have to remind yourself symbolically which side of the three dots "more" or "before" is.

OTHER CLUES AND THEIR SYMBOLS

Here are some tips on symbolizing other types of clues.

K, L, and M are male and N, O, and P are female.

You could use uppercase for one gender and lowercase for the other. Or, you could use subscript to indicate the gender categories—in other words, write down a "K" and put a little "m" for "male" at the foot of it, like this: K_M. Subscript is a good way to indicate categories. But chances are this clue comes from a game where you have more to worry about than just gender. So, instead of always using subscript to indicate categories for elements, it's helpful to use shapes. Let's say we decide that boxes represent males and circles represent females. Then, the symbol for this clue would look like this:

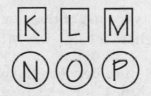

Every time you assign K, you assign him with his shape around him. That way, you never have to look back at some list, or, worse yet, the text of the game, to refresh your memory about whether K is male or female. For that matter, you should never rely on your memory for anything.

Four people choose mangoes.

$$MMMM$$

Don't symbolize this clue as 4M. This is not algebra class. The correct symbol is MMMM. This way, as you assign the elements, you can cross them out, and see exactly how many you have left.

At least one rose must be chosen.

How about this?

$$1R^+$$

The "plus" is a good way to indicate "at least."

What if you have a game with eight shelves, but only seven statues to put on them? That means you have an empty shelf, right? Right. Why not symbolize it? When writing out your list of elements, add an "X" or an "E" to symbolize it, as if it was the "empty" or "invisible" statue. This really helps you visualize the situation. For example, if a clue in this game says "The third shelf cannot be empty," instead of doing nothing with that clue, you can symbolize a "no X" next to or on top of the third shelf.

Symbolizing Drill

1. Bart cannot sit (next to) Lisa.   *Not order*   BL̶   L̶B̶

2. K always finishes somewhere ahead of D.   D̶ . . . K̶

3. If Steve and Edie serve together on same committee, Frank cannot serve on that committee.   SE ⟶ ~F   *½*

4. Two of the flowers are roses, two are daffodils, two are irises, and one is a carnation.   RR DD II C

5. The cat show finalists consist of three long-haired cats—K, L, M—and three short-haired cats—R, S, T.   K L M R S T

6. There is exactly one office between the psychiatrist's office and the bricklayer's office

7. If the guitarist performs on Monday, the drummer must perform on Tuesday.

8. The yoga class must be immediately before or immediately after the tai chi class.

Check your answers on page 54.

One final word: If you find that you cannot come up with a good symbol for a clue, don't panic and spend ten minutes thinking about it. Put an asterisk next to it. You must keep moving when you're doing games. But you must remember to go back to it when you're making deductions and each time you do a question. One forgotten clue, and the game is a lost cause.

STEP 3: DOUBLE-CHECK YOUR WORK AND MAKE DEDUCTIONS

DOUBLE CHECKING

Don't take the double-checking part of this step for granted. Read the whole setup again. Read each clue, and check your symbol. Make sure it makes sense to you. Put asterisks next to, or circle any clue you didn't symbolize. This only takes 20 seconds, but it can save your life. What if, when symbolizing an antiblock, you had forgotten to put a slash through the box, and you went through the whole game thinking it was a block? Yikes! That's what double-checking is for—to catch stuff like that. So do it.

When double-checking, here are some things to look for:

- **Do all of your symbols correspond with the clues as written?** Be especially careful with right left, before-after, and other easily confused directions. One overlooked or mis-symbolized clue can ruin the whole game.

- **Are there any clues that you couldn't symbolize?** If so, have you marked them with asterisks or a circle so that you'll remember to check them as you do each question?

DEDUCTIONS

Okay, time to talk about deductions. Blocks should be the first clues you use when making deductions. Let's say your diagram has Monday through Friday along the top, like so:

M T W R F

Now let's say one of the clues for this game is:

Roland must perform on the day immediately before the
day on which Walter performs.

First, let's symbolize it:

$$\boxed{RW}$$

Time → always left to right!

Now, it's deduction time. If Roland is immediately to the left of Walter, on which day can Roland NOT perform? If you said Friday, you're right. After all, if he did perform on Friday, where would you put Walter? Nowhere, so it's no good. So, you'd put a "not Roland" over Friday on your diagram, like so:

Rest → beginning + end of week.

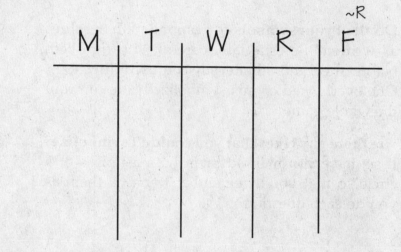

What about the other member of that block, Walter? If Roland is immediately to the left of Walter, on which day can Walter NOT perform? Right, Monday. Let's put it on the diagram:

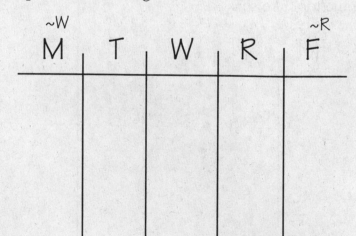

The same kinds of deductions can be made with range clues. Let's use the same Monday through Friday grid, only this time, the clue is "Lisa performs sometime before Jan performs." First, the symbol:

$$L \ldots J$$

What other restrictions can we add to the diagram? If you think we should add a "not Lisa" to Friday and a "not Jan" to Monday, you're right:

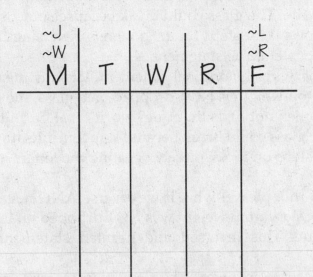

Restrictions

The whole point of using clues—blocks, range clues, and deductions—is to put as many restrictions on your diagram as possible *before even beginning the questions*. Restrictions are crucial to an effective diagram. Start answering questions by using the most restrictive elements. Elements with no restrictions are the last ones you should worry about.

Think negative. You should always think about where an element *can't* go, and mark that accordingly on your diagram. Let's say you're assigning five elements to five spaces, and you know that three of the elements are restricted from being in the fourth space. That leaves only two possible elements for that fourth space. And if a question tells you that one of those possible elements is *not* in the fourth space, then you automatically know which element *is* in the fourth space.

The Contrapositive

The contrapositive is the mandatory deduction for any "if-then" clue.

Suppose I told you that if you drop a two-ton weight on a glass, the glass would break. Is there anyone out there who could say that this *isn't* true? I didn't think so. In shorthand, you could express that as "if weight, then break" or "if w, then b."

Let's reverse the order of the statements. If the glass breaks, then a two-ton weight was dropped on it (if b, then w). Is that true? No, it *could* be, but it doesn't *have to* be. The glass could break because someone hits it with a hammer, or throws it, or steps on it. So merely reversing the order·of the letters does not yield a true statement.

Now, starting with the original statement, let's just negate both statements. If a two-ton weight is NOT dropped on a glass, the glass will NOT break (if not w, then not b). Is that true? No, it *could* be, but it doesn't *have to* be. Again, the glass could break because someone hits it with a hammer, or throws it, or steps on it. So, merely negating the letters does not yield a true statement.

Now, (drum roll, please) what if we reverse AND negate? If the glass does NOT break, a two-ton weight was NOT dropped on it. Is it true? Yes, it MUST be true. This reversed and negated statement is called the contrapositive.

The contrapositive is always the deduction to make from an if-then statement. For example, if a clue in a game said:

> If Debbie goes, then Robert goes.

you already know that you would symbolize it as

$$D \longrightarrow R$$

The deduction would be the contrapositive. In other words, you reverse the order of the elements, and negate both elements, to get this:

$$\sim R \longrightarrow \sim D$$

This is the only other statement that MUST BE TRUE. If you don't reverse *and* negate, you won't get a statement that must be true.

Here are some of the "if-then" symbols from before. Write in the contrapositives next to them in the space provided:

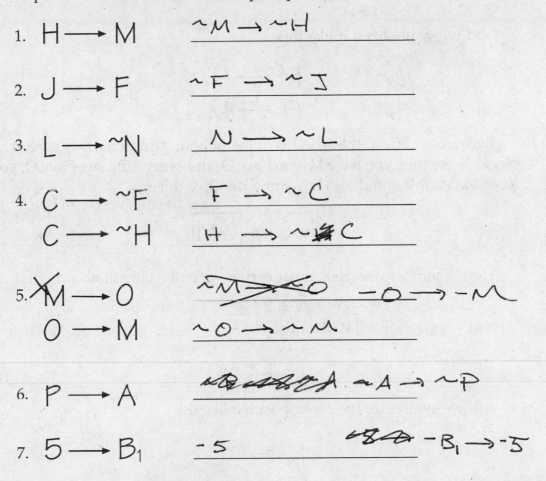

1. $H \longrightarrow M$ $\sim M \rightarrow \sim H$

2. $J \longrightarrow F$ $\sim F \rightarrow \sim J$

3. $L \longrightarrow \sim N$ $N \rightarrow \sim L$

4. $C \longrightarrow \sim F$ $F \rightarrow \sim C$

   $C \longrightarrow \sim H$ $H \rightarrow \sim C$

5. $\cancel{M} \longrightarrow O$ $\cancel{\sim M \rightarrow \sim O}$ $-O \rightarrow -M$

   $O \longrightarrow M$ $\sim O \rightarrow \sim M$

6. $P \longrightarrow A$ $\cancel{\sim A \rightarrow \sim A} \sim A \rightarrow \sim P$

7. $5 \longrightarrow B_1$ -5 $\cancel{-B} -B_1 \rightarrow -5$

Check your answers on page 54.

Linking Clues

How do you link clues? Like this: If one clues says L cannot be with T, and another clue says Q must be with T, what do you know? Can you figure something out about the relationship between Q and L? Yes. If L and T are in an antiblock, and Q and T are in a block, then Q and L must be in an antiblock. Why? Because Q brings T, and L can't be with T.

Here's another way: remember earlier we had a clue that said:

> If either mushrooms or onions is served, then both must
> be served.

and we symbolized it like this:

$$M \longrightarrow O$$
$$O \longrightarrow M$$

Because, in effect, the arrow is going in both directions, this is really a block. Every time you have M, you have O, and every time you have O, you have M. So, this could also be symbolized like this:

$$\boxed{MO} \Big/ \boxed{OM}$$

Here's another one: remember earlier we had a clue that said:

> If Liza is at the meeting, Ned cannot be at the meeting.

and we symbolized it like this:

$$L \longrightarrow \sim N$$

and we symbolize the contrapositive like this:

$$N \longrightarrow \sim L$$

Was anyone out there thinking that this is also an antiblock? Well, it is. Think about it. If L is there, N can't be, and if N is there, L cannot be. Yep, linking those clues together provides us with an antiblock, which could be symbolized like this:

Distribution

Some of the trickier Assignment Games have an extra step that we call Distribution. It's not a type of game, it's just an extra step. In a game with clues about *how many* elements go in the places (only the trickiest games will have this), distribution is an extra step you have to take when first setting it up. Think of it as an extra deduction. If you have a whole bunch of elements to put in a few places, and you don't know how many go in each place, and there are clues about the *number* of elements, like *how many* go in a certain place, you know you're dealing with distribution.

What is Distribution? Well, what if you had three cars, and you had seven people to assign to them? And what if you were told that you couldn't have more than four people in each car? What are the different ways you could "spread out" or distribute the seven people in the three cars (assuming order doesn't matter, and without repeating a set of numbers)?

Car 1	Car 2	Car 3
4	2	1
3	3	1
2	3	2

Remember, a distribution of 4-2-1 includes all permutations of those three numbers, so it includes 1-2-4, 2-1-4, 4-1-2, etc. You would just put this little chart on the side of your main diagram. In most cases, either the clues or the questions will narrow down the Distribution possibilities.

LET'S SEE IT ALL IN ACTION
Let's practice drawing a diagram, symbolizing clues, double-checking, and making deductions by looking at a game. It's tea time again (hope this looks familiar; you saw it earlier):

In a window display, there are five teapots, A, B, C, D, and E. Each teapot is a different color: red, orange, yellow, green, or purple. The display has two shelves, a left shelf and a right shelf; three teapots are displayed on the left shelf, the other two on the right shelf. The display must meet the following additional conditions:

A is displayed on the right shelf.
B is displayed on the left shelf and is not orange.
C is not displayed on a shelf where the green teapot is displayed.
E is the yellow teapot.
The orange teapot and the yellow teapot are displayed on the same shelf.

1. If C is displayed on the left shelf, which one of the following must be true?

   (A) The yellow teapot is displayed on the right shelf.
   (B) The orange teapot is displayed on the right shelf.
   (C) D is displayed on the right shelf.
   (D) D is displayed on the left shelf.
   (E) The green teapot is displayed on the left shelf.

2. Which one of the following must be true?

   (A) The yellow teapot is on the right shelf.
   (B) The red teapot is on the left shelf.
   (C) The orange teapot is on the right shelf.
   (D) The orange teapot is on the left shelf.
   (E) The green teapot is on the right shelf.

Step 1 dictates that we draw the diagram. We're assigning teapots to shelves, and we have to account for both teapot and color, so let's draw our diagram like this:

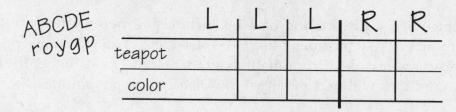

Step 2 says that we symbolize the clues. Let's do each one separately:

A is displayed on the right shelf.

Does it matter which "right" slot we put A in? Nope. These clues never made a big deal out of order within each shelf, and neither will we. Just fill in an A on a right shelf:

Next clue:

B is displayed on the left shelf and is not orange.

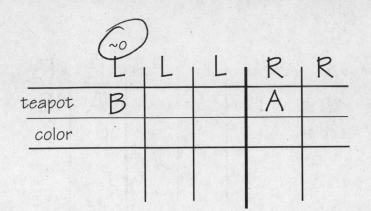

Next clue:

C is not displayed on a shelf where the green teapot is displayed.

$$C_L \longrightarrow g_R$$
$$C_R \longrightarrow g_L$$

Next clue:

E is the yellow teapot.

$$\boxed{\begin{array}{c} E \\ y \end{array}}$$

Next clue:

The orange teapot and the yellow teapot are displayed on the same shelf.

$$\boxed{O_L \; y_L} \Big/ \boxed{O_R \; y_R}$$

Now, to the deductions. First, let's take care of the contrapositives. You can put them in parentheses next to the symbolized clues, like so:

$$C_L \longrightarrow g_R \qquad (\sim g_R \longrightarrow \sim C_L)$$
$$C_R \longrightarrow g_L \qquad (\sim g_L \longrightarrow \sim C_R)$$

Now, you've got two blocks—a horizontal one and a vertical one. They involve the same element, yellow. Let's see if we can do anything. Well, the right shelf holds fewer teapots, and is therefore more restricted, so let's see if we could put those two blocks on the right shelf:

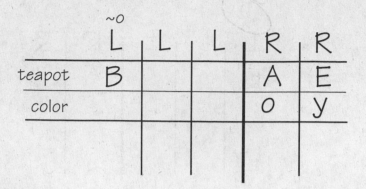

Is this okay? Check the other clues. Hmm...what about that clue about C and green? Now that the whole right shelf seems to be filled up, wouldn't that force C and green to be on the same shelf? You bet. So, this doesn't work. Those two blocks cannot go on the right shelf. Which means, what shelf are they on? The left shelf! Well, let's put 'em there:

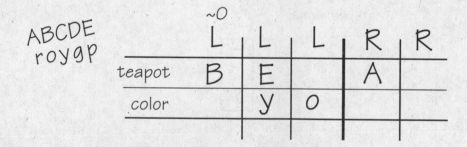

That was a huge deduction on a pretty tricky game. You linked the clues together and used those blocks and restricted places. Whatever you figure out when making deductions is true for the entire game.

Before you try those questions, let's find out more about them...

STEP 4: DECIDE QUESTION ORDER
(NOT FOR GRE CAT, BUT READ THIS ANYWAY)

There are two types of games questions: If and Which.

"**If**" questions begin with "If." Do "If" questions first. When the question says "If Q is on the third floor, which floor must X be on?" you have been given a valuable hint for that question: start by putting Q in slot 3 on your diagram. See if doing that triggers something else.

"**Which**" questions begin with "Which." Do "Which" questions after you have done "If" questions, because you can use work you've already done. You should never ever erase any work you've done. Repeat after me: I will not erase anything.

Let's look at the two questions that came with the game we just set up. Number one is an "If" question, so let's start there.

Here's our diagram again:

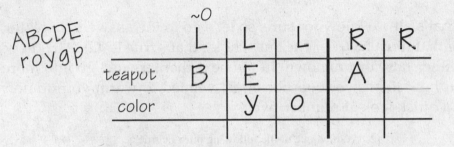

1. If C is displayed on the left shelf, which one of the following must be true?

   (A) The yellow teapot is displayed on the right shelf.
   (B) The orange teapot is displayed on the right shelf.
   (C) D is displayed on the right shelf.
   (D) D is displayed on the left shelf.
   (E) The green teapot is displayed on the left shelf.

The question wants C on the left shelf, so put it in:

	~O				
	L	L	L	R	R
teapot	B	E	C	A	
color		y	o		

Now let's see what else we know. There's only one space left in the teapot row, and one teapot left to assign. It's D. Put it in:

That's all we know for sure, so let's go to the answers. Look for something that must be true. The only choice that's true is (C). All other choices are either false or unknown. In the next chapter we'll go into more detail about how to answer questions. Just wanted to warm you up now. Let's take a quick look at number two:

2.   Which one of the following must be true?

(A)   The yellow teapot is on the right shelf.
(B)   The red teapot is on the left shelf.
(C)   The orange teapot is on the right shelf.
(D)   The orange teapot is on the left shelf.
(E)   The green teapot is on the right shelf.

Nothing to fill in on the diagram here, but since we did all that great deducing before the game started, we're ready to answer this question. If we didn't do all that work beforehand, we'd have to try out every one of these answer choices, on our diagram till we found something that worked. But we paid our dues on this game, so now let's reap the rewards. Read through the answers. See anything that we know is always true? Yes, it's (D).

Don't worry, you will have many opportunities to practice questions in the rest of the chapters of this book

Here is some general strategy for dealing with the different wording of games questions. Feel free to use it for reference throughout the book:

- On **must be true** questions, try to disprove each answer choice. The choice that's always true is the right answer. The wrong answers could be false or could be true sometimes.

- On **could be true** questions, try the answer choices. When you find a choice that's possible, that's the correct answer. The wrong answers cannot be true.

- On **must be false** questions, try each answer choice. The answer choice that cannot be true is the right answer. The wrong answers could be true.

- On **could be false** questions, try to disprove each answer choice. The choice that's not always true is the right answer. The wrong answers must be true.

- On **possible arrangement** questions (questions like "which of the following is a possible arrangement of teapots"), use Process of Elimination. Start with the most definite clue and eliminate all answer choices that violate it. Do this with each clue until you've eliminated the four incorrect answer choices.

- On **EXCEPT/CANNOT** questions, circle the except/cannot to help you remember, Then do the question in reverse. For example, if the question says, "All of the following could be true EXCEPT," eliminate every answer choice that could be true. Check every answer choice; the one that is *not* like the others is the correct answer.

- On questions that start with the word **suppose**, either a new clue is added to the original clues or one of the original clues is removed. Do these questions LAST, because the change in the rules only applies to this question, and you might have to redraw your diagram. Always remember to check all the original clues that have *not* changed.

Are "suppose" questions worth it? Well, it depends. Of course, if you're taking the GRE CAT, you can't skip a question. It's the only question on your screen and you must answer it to move on. But if you're taking the paper-and-pencil GRE or the LSAT, you might ask yourself whether you really want to re-diagram the entire game just to answer one question, when there might be one, two, or three more games in the section that you could start instead. You might wonder whether you shouldn't just fill something in on your answer sheet and move on. Here's how to make that decision:

- **Does the score range you are currently in dictate that you answer every question?** The answer for very few people would be "yes" (refer back to the pacing information in chapter 1). But if the answer is "yes," do the question.

- **Do you feel good about this game?** In other words, has it been going smoothly so far? If it has, give the "Suppose" question a shot. If it hasn't, fill in something on your answer sheet and move on.

Obviously the "Decide Question Order" step does not apply if you are taking the GRE CAT, because you don't get to do questions out of order on that test. You just have to take what they give you. So, go right to...

STEP 5: KEEP YOUR PENCIL MOVING

After you have filled in your diagram with whatever the question gives you, don't just stare anxiously at the diagram and expect to figure out the answer. Try something. Write it on the diagram. Check it against the clues, because the answers really lie there. If you're really stuck, go to the answers and use process of elimination to get rid of answers that don't work. Never stop trying things. And don't look away from your setup; stay in its "world." Momentum is a big part of doing well on games. Remember to save all work—you will be able to use it to answer other questions.

IT WON'T HURT ANYMORE

Now that we've gone into detail regarding diagrams, clues and deductions, it's your turn to try setting up different types of games. These games have the same structure as those teapot games from before. However, the cast of characters is a little different. Don't let the goofy themes distract you; the structures of these games are real. Your mission is to boil each game down to its *structure*, because that's all that matters.

First, you try setting each game up in the space provided. Then check out what we did.

Six members of the Love Boat crew—Doc, Gopher, Isaac, Julie, Merrill, and Vicki—are dancing in a row on stage on the Lido deck. The order in which they are dancing must meet the following conditions:

Isaac cannot dance next to Vicki.
Merrill cannot dance next to Julie.
Julie must dance next to Doc.

First, you try:

Our turn:

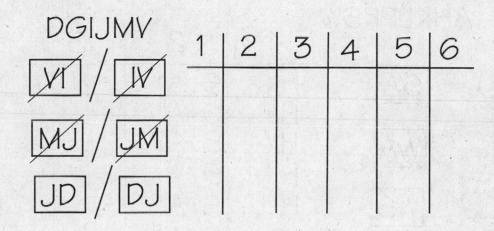

TYPE: ASSIGNMENT

Next game:

Eight philosophers—Aristotle, Hegel, Kant, Locke, Plato, Rousseau, Socrates, and Wittgenstein—are having lunch together and are sharing three pizzas. One of the pizzas will feed two philosophers, and the other two pizzas will feed three philosophers. The following conditions must be met:
Hegel will only eat the two-philosopher pizza.
Kant will not eat any of the two-philosopher pizza.
Socrates and Aristotle eat the same pizza.
Wittgenstein and Aristotle do not eat the same pizza.

First, you try:

Our turn:

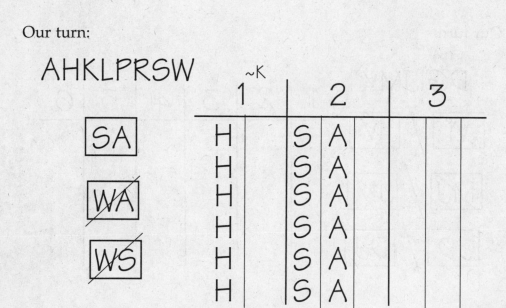

TYPE: Assignment

Since we know H eats the two-philosopher pizza, just put him in there. Since S and A eat the same pizza, they can't eat pizza 1 (no room for both of them), so put them under pizza 2 (or 3—it doesn't matter because the game doesn't distinguish between these pizzas). Notice that there are Hs, Ss and As going all the way down those columns. That way, the space is taken up, and every time we set up a question, we don't have to remember to fill them. Also notice that since the order the elements are arranged in doesn't matter, the blocks and antiblocks only have to go in one direction. That last antiblock, about W and S, was gotten by linking the SA block with

the WA antiblock.
　　Next game:

> Due to popular demand, four movies are being selected for a
> Keanu Reeves Film Festival. There are eight movies to
> choose from—*Bill and Ted's Excellent Adventure*, *Dracula*,
> *I Love You to Death*, *Johnny Mnemonic*, *Little Buddha*, *My
> Own Private Idaho*, *River's Edge*, and *Speed*. The selection
> must be made according to the following conditions:
>> *Bill and Ted's Excellent Adventure* cannot be selected
>> unless *Dracula* is also selected.
>> The festival must include *Johnny Mnemonic* or *Little
>> Buddha* or both.
>> The festival cannot include both *My Own Private Idaho*
>> and *I Love You to Death*.

First, you try:

Our turn:

BDIJLMRS

B ⟶ D

(~D ⟶ ~B)

J / L / JL

M̶I̶

	1	2	3	4	OUT

TYPE: Assignment

One letter per element, please! Did you notice the "out" column? This is crucial when diagramming a game where not every element gets assigned. The really helpful thing about the "out" column is that sometimes you can use who's out to help you figure out who's in. For example, in this game, if, when doing a question, you put four films in the "out" column, then you automatically know that the other four are "in."

Next game:

> An actor is doing a week of one-man shows. Each night of a certain week, starting Monday and ending Friday, the actor will do a soliloquy from a different Shakespearean play. The five Shakespearean characters are Hamlet, Julius Caesar, Macbeth, Othello, and Prospero. The actor will also wear a different colored pair of tights each night he performs. The five possible colors of the tights are brown, green, red, white, and yellow. The actor's schedule must conform to the following conditions:
>
>> Othello can only be portrayed on Wednesday or Friday.
>> The green tights must be worn on either the night immediately before or the night immediately after the night on which Julius Caesar is portrayed.
>> Hamlet and Macbeth must be portrayed on consecutive nights.
>> The brown tights cannot be worn while portraying Prospero.
>> The red tights must be worn earlier in the week than the white tights are worn.

First, you try:

Our turn:

H J M O P
b g r w y

		~w ~O	~O		~O	~r
		M	T	W	R	F
gJ / Jg	char.					
	color					
HM / MH	char.					
	color					
P/b	char.					
	color					

r... w

TYPE: Assignment

All you have to do when there is more than one level of elements to assign
is make two rows, one for each category. Notice that we now have both
horizontal and vertical blocks and antiblocks, depending on the relationship of the elements in question. The blocks always should look as though
they could be lifted up and placed directly on the diagram.

Notice that clues were symbolized directly on the diagram whenever
possible (like the Othello clue). Also notice the deductions drawn from the
last range clue (the red and white tights).

Next game:

> Six men—Dean, Ehrlichman, Haldeman, Liddy, Mitchell,
> and Nixon—are sitting at a round table, discussing things.
> The following is known about their seating arrangement:
>   Dean must sit next to Nixon.
>   There is to be exactly one seat between Ehrlichman and
>   Haldeman.
>   Haldeman cannot sit next to Nixon.
>   Liddy cannot sit next to both Dean and Haldeman.

First, you try:

Our turn:

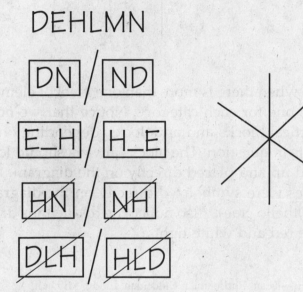

TYPE: Assignment

Notice that we didn't draw a circle. We drew an asterisk.

Because this picture isn't a grid, you'll have to redraw it for each "If" question (the questions that give you new information), because you should NEVER erase anything.

Next game:

> Six daytime talk show hosts—Geraldo, Jenny, Montel, Oprah, Ricki, and Sally—are comparing the ratings of their shows.
>> Geraldo has higher ratings than Oprah, but lower ratings than Sally.
>> Ricki has higher ratings than Montel, but lower ratings than Geraldo.
>> Jenny does not have higher ratings than Sally.

First, you try:

Our turn:

GJMORS

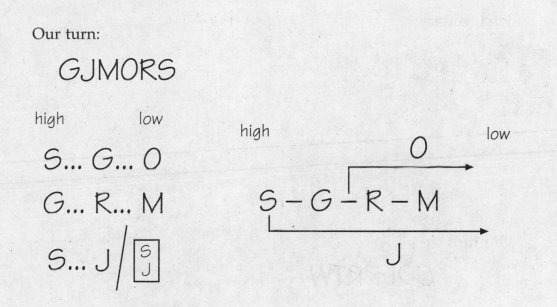

TYPE: Non-Assignment, Range

First, symbolize each clue separately, keeping it straight in terms of what you're comparing (in this case, more to less is the spectrum). Then link all the little "chains" of information to form the longest chain possible. Any element not on the main chain is called a "floater" and its range must be shown. Ranges could be extended as far as possible, which is why we use arrows. Think of those ranges as rubber bands. Any floater on a range can move back and forth along that range's arrow.

We hope you were careful about that last clue. Just because Jenny does not have higher ratings than Sally does not mean she has lower ratings. She could have the same. That's why her "range" starts *at* S, while Oprah's starts *after* G.

Next game:

> Seven crew members of the starship *Enterprise*—Crusher, Data, La Forge, Picard, Riker, Troi, and Worf—have built tunnels connecting all of their cabins. The tunnel system may only be entered and exited through a trap door located in Crusher's cabin. The following list includes all of the tunnels:
>
> There is a tunnel connecting Crusher's cabin to Data's cabin, La Forge's cabin, and Riker's cabin.
>
> There is a tunnel connecting Data's cabin and La Forge's cabin.
>
> There is a tunnel connecting Riker's cabin to Picard's cabin and to Troi's cabin.
>
> There is a tunnel connecting Troi's cabin and Worf's cabin.

First, you try:

Our turn:

CDLPRTW

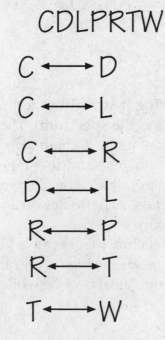

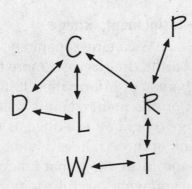

TYPE: Non-Assignment, Path/Map

Don't worry if your diagram looked a little different from this one. It doesn't make much difference where the elements are, as long as the *connections* are drawn clearly. Note that those arrows are not "if-then" arrows. They are just directional arrows.

Next game:

Kandinsky, Monet, Picasso and Vermeer are competing in a Seventies dance contest. In each round of the contest, different dances are performed. A contestant is eliminated the first time he fails to perform a dance properly. The contestants will be rearranged between rounds according to one of the following rules:

Hustle Rule: The contestant who was in third place moves in front of the contestant who was previously in first place.

Big Comb in Back Pocket Rule: The contestant who was in last place moves into the first place position.

Glitter Ball Rule: The contestant who was in third place moves in front of the contestant who was previously in second place.

If a rearrangement involves a place where a contestant has been eliminated, that rearrangement cannot occur.

If none of the rearrangements can occur, the contestants will remain in the same order as they were in the preceding round.

First, you try:

Our turn:

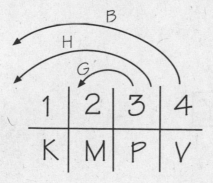

TYPE: Non-Assignment, Simon Says

There's nothing to assign, and there are rules about moving and switching. All you can do now is wait for the questions to give you orders.

OKAY, READY TO SEE THE WHOLE THING IN ACTION?

Well, turn the page!

ANSWERS TO SYMBOLS DRILLS

Drill from page 30.

1. $\boxed{\cancel{BL}}$

2. K... D

3. $\boxed{SE} \longrightarrow \sim F$

4. RRDDIIC

5. KLM rst

6. $\boxed{p-b} \Big/ \boxed{b-p}$

7. $G_M \longrightarrow D_T$

8. $\boxed{YT} \Big/ \boxed{TY}$

Drill from page 35.

1. $\sim M \longrightarrow \sim H$

2. $\sim F \longrightarrow \sim J$

3. $N \longrightarrow \sim L$

4. $F \longrightarrow \sim C, H \longrightarrow \sim C$

5. $\sim O \longrightarrow \sim M, \sim M \longrightarrow \sim O$

6. $\sim A \longrightarrow \sim P$

7. $\sim B_1 \longrightarrow \sim 5$

CHAPTER 4

A Big Ol' Game

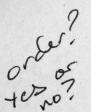

order?
yes or
no?

A TYPICAL GAME

Now it's time to make sure you've got the basic procedure down. In this chapter, we'll work through a typical game, one that could show up on an LSAT or a GRE, in excruciating detail. Here's the game:

Three shelves—1, 2, and 3—are being used to hold seven books in a student's bookcase. Each book covers a different subject—anthropology, chemistry, economics, history, physics, statistics, or zoology. No more than three books are to be displayed on a shelf. The display is subject to the following restrictions:

The history book and the anthropology book are displayed on the same shelf.

Neither the zoology book nor the chemistry book is on the same shelf as the economics book.

Neither the zoology book nor the chemistry book is on the same shelf as the physics book.

The physics book is displayed on either 1 or 2.

Each book must be displayed on one of these shelves.

1. Which one of the following is an acceptable arrangement of the books on the shelves?

	1	2	3
(A)	Zoology	Chemistry, physics, statistics	History, economics, anthropology
(B)	Zoology, economics, physics	Chemistry, statistics	History, anthropology
(C)	Economics, physics, statistics	History, zoology, chemistry	Anthropology
(D)	Economics, physics, statistics	Zoology, chemistry	History, anthropology
(E)	Economics, statistics	Zoology, chemistry	History, anthropology, physics

2. If the history and statistics books are on shelf 1, which one of the following must be true?

    (A) The zoology book is on shelf 2.
    (B) The economics book is on shelf 1.
    (C) The economics book is on shelf 3.
    (D) The chemistry book is on shelf 2.
    (E) The chemistry book is on shelf 3.

3. If the anthropology book is on shelf 2, which one of the following could be true?

    (A) The history book is on shelf 1 and the statistics book is on shelf 2.
    (B) The zoology book is on shelf 1 and the chemistry book is on shelf 2.
    (C) The zoology book is on shelf 1 and the chemistry book is on shelf 3.
    (D) The chemistry book is on shelf 1 and the statistics book is on shelf 2.
    (E) The physics book is on shelf 1 and the economics book is on shelf 2.

4. If the economics book is on shelf 2 and the physics book is on shelf 1, which one of the following must be false?

    (A) The history book is on shelf 2.
    (B) The history book is on shelf 3.
    (C) The anthropology book is on shelf 1.
    (D) The anthropology book is on shelf 2.
    (E) The statistics book is on shelf 3.

5. If the economics book is on shelf 1 and the physics book is not, which one of the following could be false?

    (A) The chemistry book is on shelf 3.
    (B) The zoology book is not on shelf 2.
    (C) The zoology book is on shelf 3.
    (D) The physics book is on shelf 2.
    (E) The history book is not on shelf 2.

6. Suppose it is no longer a requirement that the physics book be displayed either on shelf 1 or 2. If all other conditions remain true, and the physics book is on shelf 3, which one of the following must be false?

    (A) The history book is on shelf 1.
    (B) The history book is not on shelf 2.
    (C) The history book is on shelf 3.
    (D) The chemistry book is not on shelf 2.
    (E) The chemistry book is on shelf 3.

STEP 1: DECIDE ON THE APPROPRIATE DIAGRAM AND DRAW IT

Since we are assigning books to shelves, we know that this is an Assignment game, and the shelves go on top of your grid. Even if you weren't sure about that, look at the structure of the answers to question 1. It's screaming "Look! The shelves are on top! The shelves are on top!" So your diagram will look like this:

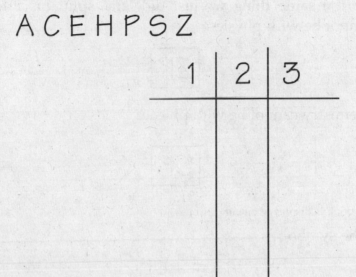

STEP 2: SYMBOLIZE THE CLUES

Let's take them one at a time:

> The history book and the anthropology book are
> displayed on the same shelf.

I'd say that's a block, wouldn't you? Here's what it looks like:

It only has to go in one direction because the order of the books on the shelf doesn't matter.

> Neither the zoology book nor the chemistry book is on
> the same shelf as the economics book.

Let's split this up into two clues, for clarity's sake. Zoology cannot be with economics:

And chemistry cannot be with economics:

Neither the zoology book nor the chemistry book is on
the same shelf as the physics book.

Let's do the same thing we just did, and split this into two clues.
Zoology cannot be with physics:

And, chemistry cannot be with physics:

The physics book is displayed on either 1 or 2.

Here's the symbol:

$$P = 1\ or\ 2$$

Each book must be displayed on one of these shelves.

This clue doesn't have much of a symbol, does it? Let's just circle it:

Each book must be displayed on one of these shelves.

Did you notice that there was a clue hiding in the setup?

No more than three books are to be displayed on a shelf.

Don't forget to underline or circle this. It's important. Don't assume that once you draw your diagram, there's nothing else in the setup you'll ever need.

STEP 3: DOUBLE-CHECK YOUR WORK AND MAKE DEDUCTIONS

"Double-check" means read every word of the setup and clues again, and check everything you've written down or circled. Just do it.

As far as deductions go, here's an easy one. If the physics book must be on either 1 or 2, where can it NOT be? Right, shelf 3.

Add that to your diagram:

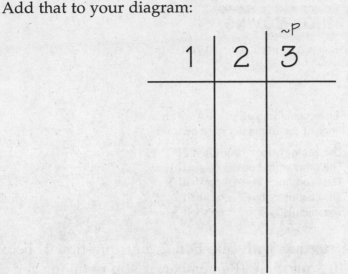

Are there any other deductions? No. Those antiblocks and blocks don't give us the exact location of any book. Time to move on to the questions.

STEP 4: DECIDE QUESTION ORDER (NOT FOR GRE CAT, BUT READ THIS ANYWAY)

If you're taking the GRE CAT, you won't have the opportunity to decide your question order. You only see one question at a time, and you can't skip around. But, for the sake of learning games, when you practice do the "If" questions first. It will help you see the game unfold. So, everyone should do the questions in the following order:

2   (Do "If" questions first!)

3   (an "If" question)

4   (another "If" question)

5   (yet another "If" question)

1   ("Which" questions should be done after "If" questions so you can use work you've already done.)

6   ("Suppose" questions should ALWAYS be done LAST because the change in rules only applies to this question.)

STEP 5: KEEP YOUR PENCIL MOVING

Stay focused, don't look away, and keep writing. Okay, let's go:

Question 2

2. If the history and statistics books are on shelf 1, which one of the following must be true?

    (A) The zoology book is on shelf 2.
    (B) The economics book is on shelf 1.
    (C) The economics book is on shelf 3.
    (D) The chemistry book is on shelf 2.
    (E) The chemistry book is on shelf 3.

Notice that we are starting with question 2, not question 1, because question 2 is the first "If" question. (Remember, if you're taking the GRE CAT, you won't have this choice in real life). Okay, first fill this information in on your diagram, like so:

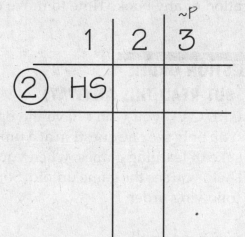

Now, what has to happen? Let's check the clues. Well, anthropology has to go on shelf 1 because of the HA block. We can't have more than three books on a shelf, so shelf 1 is full. What else do we know about the shelves? We know that we can't put the physics book on shelf 3. That means it goes on shelf 2.

Here's what we have so far:

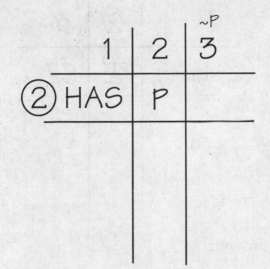

Do we have any other clues involving the physics book? Yes. We have a ZP antiblock and a CP antiblock. So where do we have to put the zoology and chemistry books?

Shelf 3:

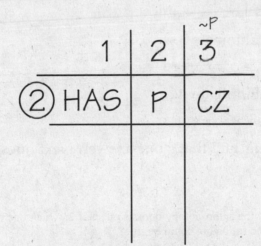

The only book we haven't placed yet is the economics book. Do we know exactly where it goes? Yes, because of the CE antiblock, it goes on shelf 2. Remember, shelf 1 is full.

```
                           ~P
              1 | 2 | 3
         ②HAS |PE | CZ
```

Let's check the answers:

(A) The zoology book is on shelf 2.

That's not true. Eliminate it.

(B) The economics book is on shelf 1.

That's not true. Eliminate it.

(C) The economics book is on shelf 3.

That's not true. Eliminate it.

(D) The chemistry book is on shelf 2.

That's not true. Eliminate it.

(E) The chemistry book is on shelf 3.

Bingo! That's true, and that's our answer. Next question, please:

Question 3

3.   If the anthropology book is on shelf 2, which one of the following could be true?

(A)   The history book is on shelf 1 and the statistics book is on shelf 2.

(B)   The zoology book is on shelf 1 and the chemistry book is on shelf 2.

(C)   The zoology book is on shelf 1 and the chemistry book is on shelf 3.

(D)   The chemistry book is on shelf 1 and the statistics book is on shelf 2.

(E)   The physics book is on shelf 1 and the economics book is on shelf 2.

Fill in the given information, like so:

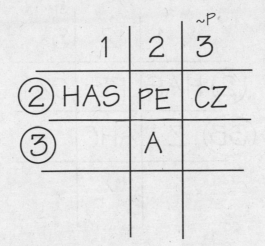

What do we know about the anthropology book? It's in a block with the history book. So, put the history book on shelf 2:

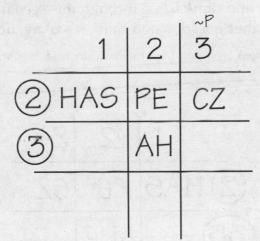

Do we know anything else for sure? Can we definitely place any book on a shelf? No. Don't be afraid when there are empty spaces on your diagram. This is a "could be true" question, so we head for the answers. If we can prove any of them wrong, we can eliminate them. Remember, four of the answers will be impossible. The remaining one will be our answer. Here are the answer choices again:

(A) The history book is on shelf 1 and the statistics book is on shelf 2.

This is easy. We already know that the history book is on shelf 2. Eliminate it.

(B) The zoology book is on shelf 1 and the chemistry book is on shelf 2.

Is this possible? Let's see:

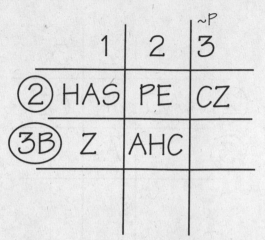

Where are you going to put the physics book? It can't go on shelf 3, and now, because of the antiblocks, it can't go on 1 or 2. So, this scenario is no good. Eliminate (B) and draw a line through this scenario (you don't want to look at it for another question and think it's okay, do you?).

(C)   The zoology book is on shelf 1 and the chemistry book is on shelf 3.

Let's try it:

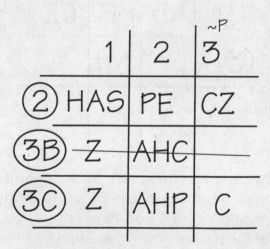

First of all, let's deal with the physics book, since it is very restricted. It will have to go on shelf 2, because of the ZP and CP antiblocks. Speaking of antiblocks, what about ZE and CE? Where will you put the economics book? There's no place for it, is there? Get rid of (C) and draw a line through this scenario.

(D) The chemistry book is on shelf 1 and the statistics book is on shelf 2.

Fill it in:

Let's deal with the physics book first again. Since no shelf can contain more than three books, shelf 2 is full, so the physics book can't go there. It can't go on shelf 1 because of the CP antiblock. And it can't go on shelf 3; that was an original clue. So, this scenario is no good. Draw a line through it and eliminate (D).

Do we have to try (E)? No. We got rid of four answers, so basically, we're done. In real life, you should just choose (E) and move on. But, since we're being extra careful here, and I know you just want to see it to make sure, let's just check (E) anyway:

(E) The physics book is on shelf 1 and the economics book is on shelf 2.

Fill it in:

The zoology and chemistry books are in antiblocks with the economics and physics books, so they go on shelf 3. That leaves us with the statistics book, which has no restrictions and therefore can go anywhere. So (E) could be true, and that's our answer.

Question 4

4. If the economics book is on shelf 2 and the physics book is on shelf 1, which one of the following must be false?

(A) The history book is on shelf 2.
(B) The history book is on shelf 3.
(C) The anthropology book is on shelf 1.
(D) The anthropology book is on shelf 2.
(E) The statistics book is on shelf 3.

Fill in the given information, like so:

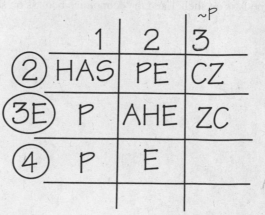

Use those antiblocks! Where do the zoology and chemistry books have to go? Right, shelf 3. Now, how about that HA block? We may not know exactly where it does go, but we do know where it can't go: shelf 3, because that would put four books on a shelf, which is no good. Here's the diagram thus far:

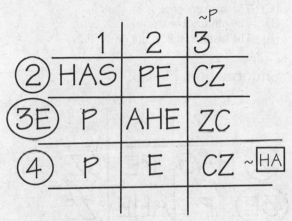

So let's check the answer choices (remember, this is a must be FALSE question. That means anything possible is wrong.):

(A) The history book is on shelf 2.

There doesn't seem to be any reason why that couldn't happen. That means it's the wrong answer.

(B) The history book is on shelf 3.

That can't happen. So that's the answer. It must be false. Do we need to check any other choices? No, not on the real test, but since we're just practicing, let's check out the others.

(C) The anthropology book is on shelf 1.

Is there any reason why the anthropology book can't be on shelf 1? No.

(D) The anthropology book is on shelf 2.

Is there any reason why the anthropology book can't be on shelf 2? No.

(E) The statistics book is on shelf 3.

Is there any reason why the statistics book can't be on shelf 3? No. Next question:

Question 5

5. If the economics book is on shelf 1 and the physics book is not, which one of the following could be false?

(A) The chemistry book is on shelf 3.
(B) The zoology book is not on shelf 2.
(C) The zoology book is on shelf 3.
(D) The physics book is on shelf 2.
(E) The history book is not on shelf 2.

Fill in the given information, like so:

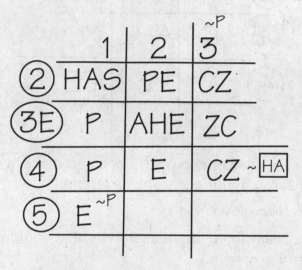

First, our restricted little physics book. It's not on shelf 1, and it can't be on shelf 3, so it must be on shelf 2. Where do the zoology and chemistry books have to go? Right, shelf 3. Now, how about that HA block? We may not know exactly where it does go, but we do know where it can't go—shelf 3, because that would put four books on a shelf, which is no good. Here's the diagram thus far:

$$
\begin{array}{c|c|c|c}
 & 1 & 2 & 3^{\sim P} \\
\hline
② & HAS & PE & CZ \\
③E & P & AHE & ZC \\
④ & P & E & CZ \sim \boxed{HA} \\
⑤ & E^{\sim P} & P & CZ \sim \boxed{HA} \\
\end{array}
$$

Let's check the answer choices. Remember, this is a "could be FALSE" question. That means anything that has to be true is wrong.

(A) The chemistry book is on shelf 3.

That has to be true. Eliminate it.

(B) The zoology book is not on shelf 2.

The zoology book is on shelf 3, so that has to be true. Eliminate it.

(C) The zoology book is on shelf 3.

That has to be true. Eliminate it.

(D) The physics book is on shelf 2.

That has to be true. Eliminate it. We know the answer must be (E). On the test, we would choose it. But for now, let's check it to make sure.

(E) The history book is not on shelf 2.

Do we know exactly where the history book is? It's either on shelf 1 or 2, but we don't know which, so (E) could be false. Bring on the next question.

Question 1

1. Which one of the following is an acceptable arrangement of the books on the shelves?

	1	2	3
(A)	Zoology	Chemistry, physics, statistics	History, economics, anthropology
(B)	Zoology, economics, physics	Chemistry, statistics	History, anthropology
(C)	Economics, physics, statistics	History, zoology, chemistry	Anthropology
(D)	Economics, physics,	Zoology, chemistry statistics	History, anthropology
(E)	Economics, statistics	Zoology, chemistry	History, anthropology, physics

This is the best kind of "Which" question. It's called a "possible arrangement" question. We don't have to put anything on our diagram. All we have to do is take each clue and hold it up against each answer choice, eliminating any choice that violates that clue.

The easiest clue to check is the one about the physics book not being on shelf 3. Are there any answer choices that violate that block? Yes, (E). Eliminate (E).

The first clue is the HA block. Are there any answer choices that violate that block? Yes, (C). Eliminate (C).

The next clue is the ZE antiblock. Are there any answer choices that violate that block? Yes, (B). Eliminate (B).

The next clue is the CE antiblock. Are there any answer choices that violate that block? Nope.

The next clue is the ZP antiblock. Are there any answer choices that violate that block? Yes, (B), but it's already gone.

The next clue is the CP antiblock. Are there any answer choices that violate that block? Yes, (A). Eliminate (A).

Which answer is left? (D), so that's our answer. Bring on the final question:

Question 6

6. Suppose it is no longer a requirement that the physics book be displayed either on shelf 1 or 2. If all other conditions remain true, and the physics book is on shelf 3, which one of the following must be false?

(A) The history book is on shelf 1.
(B) The history book is not on shelf 2.
(C) The history book is on shelf 3.
(D) The chemistry book is not on shelf 2.
(E) The chemistry book is on shelf 3.

Ah, the dreaded "Suppose" question. The kind of question that expects you to redraw your entire diagram, because it takes away one of your original conditions. This particular "Suppose" question actually isn't too bad (but this game isn't too bad, either, is it?). While they've taken away the condition about the physics book, they've told us where the physics book is. Fill it in:

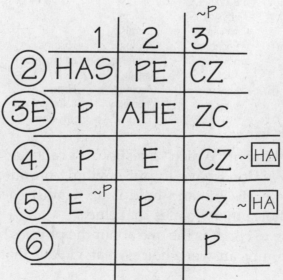

All of the other conditions still hold, but is there any other book whose position we know for sure? No. So, let's check out the answer choices (remember, this is a "must be FALSE" question. That means anything possible is wrong.):

    (A) The history book is on shelf 1.

Is this possible? Yes, so it doesn't have to be false. Eliminate it.

    (B) The history book is not on shelf 2.

This is very similar to (A). Is it possible? Yes, so it doesn't have to be false. Eliminate it.

    (C) The history book is on shelf 3.

Is this possible? Yes, so it doesn't have to be false. Eliminate it.

    (D) The chemistry book is not on shelf 2.

Is this possible? Yes, so it doesn't have to be false. Eliminate it.

    (E) The chemistry book is on shelf 3.

Not if physics is there! There's a CP antiblock. This is our answer.

SUMMARY

Congratulations! You just made it through a typical Assignment game. And here's the step-by-step approach you used, which you will use for ALL GAMES:

    Step 1: Decide on the appropriate diagram and draw it.

    Step 2: Symbolize the clues.

    Step 3: Double-check your work and make deductions.

    Step 4: Decide question order (not for GRE CAT).

    Step 5: Keep your pencil moving.

Learn it. Live it. Love it.

CHAPTER

5

The Games

WHY PRACTICE GAMES?

You're about to immerse yourself in the world of games. Why should you practice games? Because practice is the only way to get good at them. Learning the five-step process for solving games is great, but if you don't know how to use it when you take your test, it won't do you any good. Don't put yourself in that situation. Practice.

By the way, even if you're preparing for the GRE CAT, do the "If" questions first when you practice. It will help you see the game unfold.

THE EXPLANATIONS

When you check your performance on a game, don't just check the answer key. Read the explanations for each question, even if you got that question right. You may have lucked into the correct answers; make sure you understand the skill required so you can get it right the next time and every time.

THE LEVELS

These games are split into three groups: level 1, level 2, and level 3. Level 1 contains the easiest games, and level 3 contains the hardest or most time-consuming. While you're working within a particular level, think about why that game is in that level, especially if you're taking the LSAT, where part of your task is to order the games section. For example, you might notice that all Simon Says games are in level 3. That's because they tend to be either harder or more time-consuming. Other elements that make one game harder than another include:

- vague setups where you have trouble picturing the diagram

- vague clues that aren't blocks, antiblocks, or anything else that restricts elements or areas

- lots of "Which" questions and few "If" questions

HOW TO PRACTICE GAMES

Here are some tips for practicing games (we went over them in chapter 2, as well):

- **If you are taking the LSAT or the paper-and-pencil GRE, do your work in the book; don't use scrap paper.** You don't get to use it on the test, so don't grow accustomed to using it in practice.

- **If you are taking the GRE CAT, you should use the scrap paper included in the back of this book, since you get to use it for your test.** You might even want to practice these games by standing this book up, as if you were reading a computer screen, since that's what it will be like when you take your test.

Here are some tips on practicing games in general:

- Do everything in pencil, and don't erase your work.

- If a particular symbol isn't helping, or is even causing mistakes, stop using it. Try something else.

- Only practice games when you are able to give them your full attention. You have to be really careful when you do them. It's a test of how careful you can be. If you're distracted while doing them, you'll make mistakes, and you'll think it's because you "can't do them." You CAN do them, if you concentrate.

A QUESTION OF TIME

Do NOT time yourself per game. This simply isn't realistic. Different games take different amounts of time for different people. Use real full-length test sections for timing yourself (real LSATs, real GREs. By the way, if you're taking the GRE CAT, you can still use the vast number of paper-and-pencil GREs available to make up your own section). Use the games in this book to practice, learn, assess your skills, and improve.

REMEMBER!

Step 1: Decide on the appropriate diagram and draw it.

Step 2: Symbolize the clues.

Step 3: Double-check your work and make deductions.

Step 4: Decide question order (not for GRE CAT).

Step 5: Keep your pencil moving.

LEVEL 1

The games in this section have the same level of difficulty as easy LSAT games, easy GRE games, and medium GRE games. No matter how you are scoring, you should practice these games.

Example 1

A jeweler is preparing a window display of gems. There is a left display case and a right display case. In each display case, the jeweler will show three of seven gems: an amethyst, a diamond, an emerald, a garnet, an opal, a ruby and a sapphire. The gems must be shown according to the following restrictions:

The amethyst must be included in the window and must be shown in the left display case.

The diamond must be included in the window and must be shown in the right display case.

The ruby can be shown neither in the same display case as the diamond nor in the same display case as the garnet.

The emerald and the sapphire must be included in the window and must be shown together in one display case.

1. Which one of the following combinations of gems can be shown in the left display case?

    (A) Amethyst, opal, ruby
    (B) Amethyst, emerald, opal
    (C) Amethyst, garnet, sapphire
    (D) Amethyst, diamond, ruby
    (E) Diamond, emerald, sapphire

2. Which one of the following combinations of gems can be shown in the right display case?

    (A) Diamond, garnet, opal
    (B) Diamond, garnet, ruby
    (C) Diamond, ruby, sapphire
    (D) Amethyst, diamond, opal
    (E) Diamond, emerald, garnet

3. If the sapphire is shown in the left display case, which one of the following pairs of gems must be shown in the right display case?

    (A) Emerald and garnet
    (B) Garnet and opal
    (C) Amethyst and diamond
    (D) Opal and ruby
    (E) Emerald and ruby

4. If the sapphire is shown in the right display case, which one of the following pairs of gems could be shown in the left display case?

    (A) Emerald and garnet
    (B) Emerald and opal
    (C) Emerald and ruby
    (D) Garnet and ruby
    (E) Opal and ruby

Example 2

A student must see seven films for a film studies class, one film on each night of a certain week, Sunday through Saturday. The films are B, C, D, E, F, G, and H. The following conditions must be met when determining the student's schedule:

B must be seen on either the night before or the night after F is seen.

C must be seen on either the night before or the night after either E or G is seen.

H cannot be seen on the night before or on the night after D is seen.

D must be seen on Monday.

5. Which one of the following is a possible film schedule for the student, in order from Sunday to Saturday?

    (A) B, F, C, G, H, E, D
    (B) C, E, B, F, D, G, H
    (C) F, D, B, H, E, C, G
    (D) G, D, C, E, H, B, F
    (E) G, D, H, E, C, B, F

6. If B is seen on Saturday, which one of the following must be true?

    (A) F is seen on Thursday.
    (B) C is seen on Tuesday.
    (C) H is seen on Thursday.
    (D) E is seen on Wednesday.
    (E) G is seen on Sunday.

7. If G is seen on Thursday, E must be seen on

    (A) Sunday
    (B) Tuesday
    (C) Wednesday
    (D) Friday
    (E) Saturday

8. If C is seen on Saturday, which one of the following must be true?

    (A) G is seen on Friday.
    (B) H is seen on Thursday.
    (C) F is seen on Wednesday.
    (D) B is seen on Tuesday.
    (E) E is seen on Sunday.

9. Which one of the following is a night on which H could be seen?

    (A) Sunday
    (B) Tuesday
    (C) Wednesday
    (D) Friday
    (E) Saturday

Example 3

A communications system involves sending electronic mail to exactly four computer terminals: F, G, H, and J. Electronic mail travels from one computer terminal directly to another computer terminal only as follows:

> From F to G
> From F to H
> From F to J
> From J to F
> From G to H
> From H to G
> From G to J
> From J to H

A single direct path going in one direction from one computer terminal to another is referred to as a pathway.

10. If a piece of electronic mail is to travel from H to G over as few pathways as possible, it must travel in which one of the following ways?

   (A) Directly from H to G
   (B) Via F but no other computer terminal
   (C) Via J but no other computer terminal
   (D) Via F and J, in that order
   (E) Via J and F, in that order

11. Which one of the following is a complete and accurate list of computer terminals to which a piece of electronic mail can be sent along exactly one pathway from J?

   (A) F
   (B) H
   (C) F, H
   (D) G, H
   (E) F, G, H

12. Which one of the following sequences of pathways is a path over which a piece of electronic mail could travel from G back to G?

   (A) From G to F, from F to G
   (B) From G to H, from H to F, from F to J, from J to G
   (C) From G to H, from H to J, from J to F, from F to G
   (D) From G to J, from J to F, from F to H, from H to G
   (E) From G to J, from J to H, from H to F, from F to G

13. If all of the pathways in the system are equal in length, and if messages always travel along the shortest possible path, then the longest path any piece of electronic mail travels in the system is the path from

   (A) G to F
   (B) H to F
   (C) H to J
   (D) J to F
   (E) J to G

14. If certain restricted pieces of electronic mail are allowed to travel from one terminal to another only if travel can be completed by using a single pathway, and if an addition of one pathway is to be made to the system so that such restricted pieces of electronic mail can be sent from each computer terminal to at least two others and also be received by each computer terminal from at least two others, then that addition must be from

   (A) G to F
   (B) H to F
   (C) H to J
   (D) J to F
   (E) J to G

Example 4

An artist has exactly seven paintings—T, U, V, W, X, Y, and Z—from which she must choose exactly five to be in an exhibit. Any combination is acceptable provided it meets the following conditions:

If T is chosen, X cannot be chosen.
If U is chosen, Y must also be chosen.
If V is chosen, X must also be chosen.

15. Which one of the following is an acceptable combination of paintings for inclusion in the exhibit?

    (A) T, U, V, X, Y
    (B) T, U, V, Y, Z
    (C) T, W, X, Y, Z
    (D) U, V, W, Y, Z
    (E) U, V, W, X, Y

16. If the artist chooses painting V to be included among the paintings in the exhibit, which one of the following must be true of that combination of paintings?

    (A) T is not chosen.
    (B) Y is not chosen.
    (C) U is chosen.
    (D) W is chosen.
    (E) Z is chosen.

17. If painting T is chosen to be among the paintings included in the exhibit, which one of the following cannot be chosen to be among the paintings included in the exhibit?

    (A) U
    (B) V
    (C) W
    (D) Y
    (E) Z

18. If the artist does not choose painting Z for the exhibit, which one of the following also cannot be chosen?

    (A) T
    (B) U
    (C) V
    (D) W
    (E) X

19. Which one of the following substitutions can the artist always make without violating the restrictions affecting the combination of paintings, given that the painting mentioned first was not, and the painting mentioned second was, originally going to be chosen?

    (A) T replaces V.
    (B) U replaces Y.
    (C) V replaces X.
    (D) W replaces Y.
    (E) Z replaces W.

Example 5

A chef has prepared six entrees—U, V, W, X, Y, and Z—to be served, one per night, in a certain week, starting Monday and ending Saturday. The order in which the entrees are to be served must meet the following conditions:

The entrees U, V, and W, no matter what their order relative to each other, cannot be served on consecutive nights.

The entrees X, Y, and Z, no matter what their order relative to each other, cannot be served on consecutive nights.

U must be served earlier than in the week than Y is served.

V can be served neither on Monday nor on Saturday.

Z can be served neither immediately before nor immediately after V is served.

20. Which one of the following could be the order, from first to last, in which the entrees are served?

    (A) U, V, X, Y, Z, W
    (B) U, X, Z, W, Y, V
    (C) W, V, Z, U, Y, X
    (D) X, V, W, Z, U, Y
    (E) Z, X, V, Y, W, U

21. If Z is served on Wednesday, which one of the following must be true?

    (A) U is served on Monday
    (B) V is served on Friday.
    (C) W is served on Thursday.
    (D) X is served on Saturday.
    (E) Y is served on Saturday.

22. If Y is served on Wednesday, and Z is served on Thursday, then which one of the following must be true?

    (A) U is served on Tuesday.
    (B) V is served on Friday.
    (C) W is served on Friday.
    (D) W is served on Monday.
    (E) X is served on Monday.

23. If W is served on Monday, and U is served on Friday, which one of the following must be true?

    (A) X is served on Wednesday.
    (B) Z is served on Thursday.
    (C) V is served on the day immediately before the day on which U is served.
    (D) W is served on the day immediately before the day on which Z is served.
    (E) X is served on the day immediately before the day on which V is served.

24. If X is served on the day immediately after the day on which Y is served and immediately before the day on which W is served, then which one of the following could be true?

    (A) U is served on the day immediately before the day on which Y is served.
    (B) U is served on the day immediately before the day on which Z is served.
    (C) W is served on the day immediately before the day on which V is served.
    (D) W is served on the day immediately before the day on which Z is served.
    (E) Z is served on the day immediately before the day on which Y is served.

25. If W is served on Wednesday, any of the following could be the entree served on Thursday EXCEPT

    (A) U
    (B) V
    (C) X
    (D) Y
    (E) Z

Example 6

Eight guards—Stoddard, Thorpe, Udell, Vaughn, Westbrook, Xavier, Yates, and Zacharias—are guarding a valuable gem. They are stationed around the gem, equally spaced, in a circular formation. The following is known about their positions:

> Westbrook and Xavier must be stationed next to each other.
> Zacharias and Udell must be stationed next to each other.
> Stoddard must be stationed directly across the circle from Yates.

26. All of the following guards could be stationed immediately next to Udell EXCEPT

    (A) Stoddard
    (B) Thorpe
    (C) Vaughn
    (D) Xavier
    (E) Yates

27. Each of the following statements must be false EXCEPT

    (A) Thorpe is stationed next to Vaughn.
    (B) Udell is stationed next to Vaughn.
    (C) Udell is stationed next to Xavier.
    (D) Westbrook is stationed next to Zacharias.
    (E) Xavier is stationed next to Zacharias.

28. If Stoddard is stationed next to Zacharias, each of the following could be true EXCEPT

    (A) Stoddard is stationed next to Xavier.
    (B) Udell is stationed next to Thorpe.
    (C) Udell is stationed next to Yates.
    (D) Westbrook is stationed next to Yates.
    (E) Yates is stationed next to Xavier.

29. If Udell and Westbrook are each stationed next to Yates, which one of the following persons could be stationed directly across the circle from Udell?

    (A) Stoddard
    (B) Thorpe
    (C) Xavier
    (D) Yates
    (E) Zacharias

30. If Thorpe and Zacharias are each stationed next to Stoddard, which one of the following must be true?

    (A) Thorpe is stationed across from Vaughn.
    (B) Thorpe is stationed next to Westbrook.
    (C) Thorpe is stationed next to Xavier.
    (D) Udell is stationed next to Westbrook.
    (E) Udell is stationed next to Yates.

31. If Stoddard is stationed next to Zacharias, and if Xavier is stationed next to Yates, which one of the following people must be stationed directly across from Xavier?

    (A) Stoddard
    (B) Udell
    (C) Westbrook
    (D) Yates
    (E) Zacharias

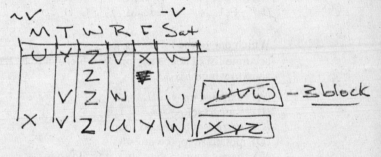

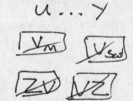

Example 7

Eight spices—F, G, H, J, K, L, M, N—are being divided among exactly three soups—carrot soup, potato soup, and tomato soup. The carrot soup and the potato soup will each have exactly three spices added to them; the tomato soup will have exactly two spices added to it. The following conditions apply:

· F must be added to the carrot soup.
· G must be added to the tomato soup.
· Neither G nor K can be added to the same soup as M.
· J cannot be added to the same soup as N.
· If H is added to the carrot soup, N must also be added to the carrot soup.

32. Which one of the following is an acceptable assignment of spices to the three soups?

	carrot	potato	tomato
(A)	F, H, M	J, K, L	G, N
(B)	F, H, N	G, J, M	K, L
(C)	F, K, L	J, M, N	G, H
(D)	F, L, N	H, J, M	G, K
(E)	F, L, N	J, K, M	G, H

33. Which one of the following is a complete and accurate list of soups any one of which could be the soup to which J is added?

(A) carrot soup
(B) tomato soup
(C) carrot soup, tomato soup
(D) potato soup, tomato soup
(E) carrot soup, potato soup, tomato soup

34. If L is added to the carrot soup, which one of the following is a spice that must be added to the potato soup?

(A) H
(B) J
(C) K
(D) M
(E) N

35. If L is added to the tomato soup, each of the following is a pair of spices that can be added to the carrot soup EXCEPT

(A) M and N
(B) K and N
(C) J and M
(D) J and K
(E) H and N

36. If H is added to the tomato soup, which one of the following is a spice that must be added to the potato soup?

(A) J
(B) K
(C) L
(D) M
(E) N

37. Which one of the following must be true?

(A) If H and L are added to potato soup, J is added to tomato soup.
(B) If J and K are added to carrot soup, H is added to tomato soup.
(C) If J and K are added to carrot soup, N is added to tomato soup.
(D) If J and L are added to carrot soup, K is added to tomato soup.
(E) If M and N are added to potato soup, L is added to potato soup.

Example 8

A certain race involves nine athletes: King, Leighton, Maynard, Nguyen, Oakley, Phelan, Quigley, Reilly, and Shea.

Oakley and Reilly run at the same time as each other, and no one else runs at that time.

Leighton and Phelan run at the same time as each other, and no one else runs at that time.

No other athlete runs at the same time as another athlete.

Nguyen runs before King.

Quigley runs before Maynard.

Maynard runs after Reilly but before Nguyen.

Phelan runs after both Shea and King.

King runs before Shea.

38. Who are the last two athletes to run?

   (A) Nguyen and Shea
   (B) King and Phelan
   (C) King and Leighton
   (D) Phelan and Leighton
   (E) Shea and King

39. Exactly how many athletes run before Shea?

   (A) 6
   (B) 5
   (C) 4
   (D) 3
   (E) 2

40. Which one of the following must be true?

   (A) Maynard is the first athlete to run.
   (B) Quigley is the first athlete to run.
   (C) Oakley and Reilly are the first two athletes to run.
   (D) Quigley and Oakley are the first two athletes to run.
   (E) Either Quigley is the first athlete to run or Oakley and Reilly are the first two athletes to run.

41. Suppose each athlete starts running at the top of an hour. If Nguyen starts running at 1:00 pm, what is the earliest that Phelan can start running?

   (A) 1:00 pm
   (B) 2:00 pm
   (C) 3:00 pm
   (D) 4:00 pm
   (E) 5:00 pm

Example 9

Six offices in a publishing company are on the same floor, which is laid out as follows:

101	102
103	104
105	106

The eight employees who could share these offices are: four editors, two proofreaders, and two graphic artists. The locations of these employees are subject to the following conditions:

No employee is in more than one of the offices.
None of the offices contains more than one proofreader, and none contains more than one graphic artist.
None of the offices contains both a proofreader and a graphic artist.
Each proofreader is located in an office that contains at least one editor.
The graphic artists are located in two offices that are not directly across from, to the left of, or to the right of each other.
Office 103 contains a graphic artist, and office 106 contains a proofreader.

42. Which one of the following could be true?

   (A) Office 105 contains a graphic artist.
   (B) Office 106 contains a graphic artist.
   (C) Office 102 contains a proofreader.
   (D) Office 103 contains a proofreader.
   (E) Office 103 contains an editor.

43. Which one of the following could be true?

   (A) Office 101 contains exactly one editor.
   (B) Office 101 contains exactly one graphic artist.
   (C) Office 102 contains exactly one proofreader.
   (D) Office 105 contains exactly one graphic artist.
   (E) Office 106 contains exactly one graphic artist.

44. Which one of the following is a complete and accurate list of the offices any one of which could contain the proofreader that is not in office 106?

   (A) 101, 104
   (B) 102, 104
   (C) 104, 105
   (D) 101, 104, 105
   (E) 101, 102, 104, 105

45. If each of the six offices contains at least one of the eight employees, then which one of the following must be true?

   (A) There is a proofreader in office 101.
   (B) There is an editor in office 102.
   (C) There is an editor in office 103.
   (D) There is an editor in office 104.
   (E) There is a proofreader in office 104.

46. In which one of the following offices must there be fewer than three editors?

   (A) 101
   (B) 102
   (C) 104
   (D) 105
   (E) 106

47. If one of the offices contains exactly two editors and exactly one graphic artist, then which one of the following lists three offices that might, among them, contain no editor?

   (A) 101, 103, 105
   (B) 101, 104, 105
   (C) 102, 103, 105
   (D) 102, 104, 106
   (E) 104, 105, 106

Example 10

In a shelving unit, there are exactly eight shelves, arranged vertically and numbered consecutively 1 (bottom), through 8 (top). Exactly six vases—B, C, D, F, G, and H—are to be placed on the shelves according to the following conditions:

No more than one vase can be placed on any shelf.
B must be placed on a lower-numbered shelf than G.
C and H, not necessarily in that order, must be placed on shelves immediately above or below each other.
Any shelf immediately above or below the shelf on which F is placed must remain empty.

48. If shelves 1 through 4 all hold vases, which one of the following could be the four vases, in order from shelf 1 to shelf 4, on those four shelves?

    (A) C, B, G, D
    (B) C, H, B, F
    (C) D, B, G, H
    (D) D, G, H, C
    (E) F, B, G, C

49. If D is on shelf 2 and F is on shelf 5, then G must be on shelf

    (A) 3
    (B) 4
    (C) 5
    (D) 6
    (E) 7

50. If shelves 3 and 7 are empty and G is on shelf 5, which one of the following must be true?

    (A) B is on shelf 1.
    (B) C is on shelf 1.
    (C) D is on shelf 6.
    (D) D is on shelf 8.
    (E) F is on shelf 2.

51. If B is on the only shelf between the two empty shelves, which one of the following must be true?

    (A) B is on shelf 6.
    (B) F is on shelf 1.
    (C) G is on a shelf immediately above or below an empty shelf.
    (D) Shelf 3 is empty.
    (E) Shelf 5 is empty.

52. If F is on shelf 2 and B is on shelf 7, then D could be on shelf

    (A) 1
    (B) 3
    (C) 5
    (D) 6
    (E) 8

53. If F is on shelf 6, then any of the following could be true EXCEPT:

    (A) B is on shelf 3.
    (B) C is on shelf 8.
    (C) D is on shelf 8.
    (D) G is on shelf 2.
    (E) H is on shelf 4.

54. If C and H are on the only two shelves between the two empty shelves, then D could be on any of the following shelves EXCEPT shelf

    (A) 1
    (B) 3
    (C) 4
    (D) 7
    (E) 8

LEVEL 2

The games in this section have the same level of difficulty as medium LSAT games and difficult GRE games. The same procedure still applies though:

Step 1: Decide on the appropriate diagram and draw it.

Step 2: Symbolize the clues.

Step 3: Double-check your work and make deductions.

Step 4: Decide question order (not for GRE CAT).

Step 5: Keep your pencil moving.

Example 1

A night club is scheduling its early and late shows for Thursday, Friday, Saturday, and Sunday of a certain week. Each show will feature exactly one of the following five bands: The Night Owls, The Parrots, The Quiet Men, The Right Stuff, and The Wobbles.

No band will be featured during a late show more than once during the week.

No band will be featured during an early show more than once during the week.

On Thursday, only The Quiet Men, The Right Stuff, or The Wobbles will be featured.

On Friday, only The Night Owls or The Wobbles will be featured.

On Saturday, only The Parrots, The Quiet Men, The Right Stuff, or The Wobbles will be featured.

On Sunday, only The Parrots, The Quiet Men, or The Wobbles will be featured.

The early show and the late show cannot feature the same band on the same night.

The Wobbles are featured on the late show on Sunday.

1. Which one of the following statements must be true?

   (A) The Right Stuff is featured during the early show on Thursday.
   (B) The Wobbles are featured during the early show on Friday.
   (C) The Quiet Men are featured during the early show on Saturday.
   (D) The Quiet Men are featured during the late show on Thursday.
   (E) The Parrots are featured during the late show on Saturday.

2. It CANNOT be true that, during the week, both the early show and the late show feature which one of the following bands?

   (A) The Night Owls
   (B) The Parrots
   (C) The Quiet Men
   (D) The Right Stuff
   (E) The Wobbles

3. If The Right Stuff is featured during the early show on Thursday, then which one of the following statements must be true?

   (A) The Parrots are featured during the early show on Saturday.
   (B) The Quiet Men are featured during the early show on Sunday.
   (C) The Quiet Men are featured during the late show on Thursday.
   (D) The Parrots are featured during the late show on Saturday.
   (E) The Right Stuff is featured during the late show on Saturday.

4. Which one of the following statements could be true?

   (A) Neither The Quiet Men nor The Right Stuff is featured during the early show on Thursday.
   (B) Neither The Quiet Men nor The Right Stuff is featured during the early show on Saturday.
   (C) Neither The Parrots nor The Quiet Men are featured during the early show on Sunday.
   (D) Neither The Quiet Men nor The Right Stuff is featured during the late show on Thursday.
   (E) Neither The Parrots, nor The Quiet Men, nor The Right Stuff is featured during the late show on Saturday.

5. If The Right Stuff is never featured during a late show, then which one of the following statements must be false?

(A) The Right Stuff is featured during the early show on Thursday.

(B) The Right Stuff is featured during the early show on Saturday.

(C) The Parrots are featured during the early show on Sunday.

(D) The Quiet Men are featured during the late show on Thursday.

(E) The Parrots are featured during the late show on Saturday.

6. Which one of the following statements could be true?

(A) The Quiet Men are featured during the early show on Thursday and The Right Stuff is featured during the late show on Saturday.

(B) The Right Stuff is featured during the early show on Saturday and The Quiet Men are featured during the early show on Sunday.

(C) The Quiet Men are featured during the early show on Saturday and The Quiet Men are featured during the late show on Thursday.

(D) The Right Stuff is featured during the early show on Saturday and The Quiet Men are featured during the late show on Thursday.

(E) The Quiet Men are featured during the early show on Sunday and The Quiet Men are featured during the late show on Saturday.

Example 2

On the third floor of a professional building, there are four offices on one side of the hall, labeled A, C, E, and G, and four offices on the opposite side of the hall, labeled consecutively B, D, F, and H. Offices B, D, F, and H face offices A, C, E, and G, respectively. Each office will belong to exactly one of three types of professionals—psychologists, lawyers, or orthodontists—according to the following conditions:

Adjacent offices must belong to different types of professionals.
No lawyer's office faces another lawyer's office.
Every psychologist's office has at least one orthodontist's office adjacent to it.
Office C is a psychologist's office.
Office F is a lawyer's office.

7. Any of the following could be an orthodontist's office EXCEPT office

    (A) A
    (B) B
    (C) D
    (D) G
    (E) H

8. If there is one psychologist's office directly opposite another psychologist's office, which one of the following could be true?

    (A) Office H is a psychologist's office.
    (B) Office G is a lawyer's office.
    (C) Office D is an orthodontist's office.
    (D) Office B is a lawyer's office.
    (E) Office A is a psychologist's office.

9. If office D is an orthodontist's office, then it could be true that office

    (A) A is an orthodontist's office
    (B) B is an orthodontist's office
    (C) E is a psychologist's office
    (D) G is an orthodontist's office
    (E) H is a psychologist's office

10. On the third floor, there could be exactly

    (A) one psychologist's office
    (B) one orthodontist's office
    (C) two orthodontist's offices
    (D) four psychologist's offices
    (E) five psychologist's offices

11. If no office occupied by a certain professional faces an office occupied by a professional of the same type, then it must be true that office

    (A) A is a lawyer's office
    (B) A is an orthodontist's office
    (C) B is a psychologist's office
    (D) B is a lawyer's office
    (E) D is an orthodontist's office

12. If the condition requiring office F to be a lawyer's office is no longer true but all other original conditions remain the same, then any of the following could be an accurate list of the professionals occupying offices B, D, F, and H, respectively, EXCEPT:

    (A) psychologist, lawyer, psychologist, orthodontist
    (B) lawyer, psychologist, orthodontist, lawyer
    (C) lawyer, orthodontist, psychologist, lawyer
    (D) orthodontist, psychologist, orthodontist, lawyer
    (E) orthodontist, lawyer, psychologist, orthodontist

Example 3

A zoo uses a tram to connect the seven different animal areas. There are two-way roads connecting each of the following pairs of points: 1 with 2, 1 with 3, 1 with 5, 2 with 6, 3 with 7, 5 with 6, and 6 with 7. There are also one-way roads going from 2 to 4, from 3 to 2, and from 4 to 3. There are no other roads in the network, and the roads in the network do not intersect.

When traveling from one area to another, the tram must take the route that for the whole trip passes through the fewest of the points 1 through 7, counting a point twice if the tram passes through it twice.

The pandas are at point 3. The tigers are at point 1, the gorillas are at point 5, and the birds are at point 4. The zebras are at point 2, the lions are at point 6, and the reptiles are at point 7.

13. If the tram starts at the tigers and goes to the reptiles, the first intermediate point on the route must be

   (A) 2
   (B) 3
   (C) 5
   (D) 6
   (E) 7

14. If, starting from the pandas, the tram goes to the tigers and the birds, (in either order), and ends up at the reptiles, the first two points on the route must be

   (A) 1 and 2
   (B) 1 and 3
   (C) 2 and 1
   (D) 2 and 4
   (E) 4 and 2

15. If, starting from the gorillas, the tram goes to the tigers or the birds (whichever stop requires the route go through the fewest number of points) and then goes to the reptiles, the first two points on the route must be

   (A) 1 and 2
   (B) 1 and 3
   (C) 4 and 2
   (D) 6 and 2
   (E) 6 and 4

16. If the tram makes a trip starting at the reptiles, going to the birds, and then ending at the lions, the first two points on the route could be

   (A) 3 and 1
   (B) 3 and 4
   (C) 4 and 2
   (D) 6 and 2
   (E) 6 and 5

Example 4

An automobile company is showing five vehicles—a family car, a pickup truck, a recreational vehicle, a sports car, and a van—on one night for a promotional event. Each vehicle must be a different color—black, green, orange, tan, or white. The following restrictions apply:

The white vehicle is shown fourth.

The black vehicle and the green vehicle are, in either order, shown immediately before and after the sports car.

There are exactly two vehicles between the recreational vehicle and the green vehicle.

The van is shown after the pickup truck.

17. Which one of the following is a possible order of vehicle colors?

	First	Second	Third	Fourth	Fifth
(A)	black	green	orange	white	tan
(B)	green	orange	tan	white	black
(C)	green	white	black	tan	orange
(D)	orange	tan	green	white	black
(E)	tan	orange	black	white	green

18. The sports car must be

(A) shown immediately before or after the family car

(B) shown immediately before or after the pickup truck

(C) separated by exactly one vehicle from the pickup truck

(D) separated by exactly one vehicle from the recreational vehicle

(E) separated by exactly one vehicle from the van

19. If the recreational vehicle is shown second, which one of the following assignments must be made?

	Color	Shown
(A)	black	first
(B)	green	fifth
(C)	orange	first
(D)	orange	third
(E)	tan	fifth

20. Which one of the following is a complete and accurate list of vehicles each of which could be black?

(A) family car, pickup truck

(B) sports car, van

(C) family car, pickup truck, recreational vehicle

(D) family car, pickup truck, van

(E) pickup truck, sports car, van

21. If the pickup truck is tan, then it must be true that

(A) the green vehicle is shown first.

(B) the orange vehicle is shown second.

(C) the family car is white.

(D) the recreational vehicle is black.

(E) the sports car is orange.

22. If the family car is tan, which one of the following could represent the order in which the vehicles are shown?

	First	Second	Third	Fourth	Fifth
(A)	family car	recreational vehicle	pickup truck	sports car	van
(B)	family car	pickup truck	recreational vehicle	van	sports car
(C)	family car	van	sports car	pickup truck	recreational vehicle
(D)	pickup truck	recreational vehicle	family car	sports car	van
(E)	pickup truck	van	recreational vehicle	sports car	family car

Example 5

The student jury at the university will consist of exactly five members, one of whom will be its foreman. The members will be appointed from among a group of five graduate students—B, C, D, E, and F—and a group of four undergraduate students—M, N, O, and P. The following conditions must be met:

    The student jury must include at least two appointees from each group.

    The foreman must be a member belonging to the group from which exactly two members are appointed.

    If B is appointed, N must be appointed.

    If C is appointed, E must be appointed.

    If either D or F is appointed, the other must also appointed.

    F and M cannot both be appointed.

23. Which one of the following is an acceptable selection of members for the student jury?

    (A) B, C, N, O, P
    (B) B, D, E, M, N
    (C) B, M, N, O, P
    (D) D, E, F, N, P
    (E) D, F, M, N, P

24. Which one of the following lists three members who could be appointed together for the student jury?

    (A) B, C, D
    (B) B, C, F
    (C) B, D, F
    (D) C, D, E
    (E) C, D, F

25. If F is the foreman of the student jury, which one of the following is among the people who must also be on the student jury?

    (A) B
    (B) C
    (C) E
    (D) M
    (E) O

26. If B is the foreman of the student jury, which one of the following is among the people who must also be on the student jury?

    (A) C
    (B) E
    (C) M
    (D) O
    (E) P

27. If B is appointed, any one of the following people could be the foreman of the student jury EXCEPT

    (A) C
    (B) E
    (C) M
    (D) N
    (E) P

28. If neither B nor E is appointed to the student jury, which one of the following can be true?

    (A) C is appointed.
    (B) M is appointed.
    (C) D is the foreman.
    (D) N is the foreman.
    (E) P is the foreman.

29. If the foreman of the student jury is to be an undergraduate student, which one of the following must be true?

    (A) If C is appointed, N is also appointed.
    (B) If C is appointed, O is also appointed.
    (C) If D is appointed, B is also appointed.
    (D) If D is appointed, N is also appointed.
    (E) If D is appointed, O is also appointed.

30. The student jury must include at least one member from which one of the following pairs?

    (A) B, M
    (B) C, D
    (C) E, N
    (D) F, M
    (E) O, P

Example 6

Four cities—Boston, Chicago, Los Angeles, and New York—are to be visited for a promotional tour of a new weight-loss program. There are six stops on the tour. On each stop, exactly one of the cities is visited, and cities can be visited more than once. The schedule of the visits must meet the following conditions:

Each city is visited at least once.

No city is visited twice in a row.

Boston is not visited first.

New York is visited third or sixth or both, and it may also be visited on other days.

If Chicago is visited first, then New York is not visited sixth.

31. Which one of the following could be the schedule of the visits for one week, for the days of first through sixth, respectively?

    (A) Chicago, Boston, New York, Los Angeles, Chicago, Chicago
    (B) Chicago, Boston, New York, Los Angeles, Boston, New York
    (C) Los Angeles, Boston, Chicago, New York, Los Angeles, Boston
    (D) Los Angeles, Chicago, New York, Boston, Los Angeles, Boston
    (E) Los Angeles, Chicago, New York, Los Angeles, New York, Chicago

32. Which one of the following could be true of one week's schedule of visits?

    (A) Boston is visited both third and sixth.
    (B) Chicago is visited both first and third.
    (C) New York is visited both second and fifth.
    (D) Chicago is visited first and New York is visited fourth.
    (E) New York is visited third and Chicago is visited sixth.

33. If during one week New York is visited third and sixth only, which one of the following must be true of that week?

    (A) Boston is visited second.
    (B) Chicago is visited fifth.
    (C) Los Angeles is visited first.
    (D) Boston is visited exactly two times.
    (E) Los Angeles is visited exactly two times.

34. If Chicago is visited first and sixth only, which one of the following must be true?

    (A) One other city besides Chicago is visited exactly twice.
    (B) The city that is visited third is not visited fifth.
    (C) Los Angeles is visited immediately before Boston is visited.
    (D) Either Boston or Los Angeles is visited fifth.
    (E) Either Los Angeles or New York is visited second.

35. Which one of the following CANNOT be true of one week's schedule of visits?

    (A) Boston is visited second and Chicago is visited fifth.
    (B) Chicago is visited first and New York is visited second.
    (C) Chicago is visited first and New York is visited fifth.
    (D) Los Angeles is visited first and New York is visited second.
    (E) Los Angeles is visited second and New York is visited fifth.

36. If Boston is visited exactly twice but that city is visited neither second nor third, which one of the following could be true?

    (A) One city is visited exactly three times.
    (B) Three cities are visited exactly one time each.
    (C) New York is not visited immediately before Boston is visited.
    (D) Chicago is visited third.
    (E) New York is visited fifth.

Example 7

Nine swimmers—Angus, Bridget, Caleb, Darla, Eugene, Faith, Garth, Hannah, and Ives—are each placed in one of three groups. The three fastest swimmers are placed in the Shark group; the three slowest swimmers are placed in the Guppy group. The remaining three are placed in the Minnow group. Each group has exactly three swimmers.

Darla swims faster than Bridget.
Bridget swims faster than both Eugene and Faith. *Ambig*
Eugene swims faster than Hannah.
Hannah swims faster than Caleb.
Caleb swims faster than Ives.
Faith swims faster than both Angus and Garth. *Ambig*

37. How many different combinations of swimmers could form the Shark group?

    (A) 1
    (B) 2
    (C) 3
    (D) 4
    (E) 6

38. Which one of the following swimmers could be in the Minnow group but cannot be in the Guppy group?

    (A) Angus
    (B) Bridget
    (C) Eugene
    (D) Faith
    (E) Ives

39. Which one of the following swimmers could be placed in any one of the three groups?

    (A) Angus
    (B) Eugene
    (C) Faith
    (D) Garth
    (E) Ives

40. The composition of each group can be completely determined if which one of the following pairs of swimmers is known to be in the Minnow group?

    (A) Angus and Faith
    (B) Angus and Hannah
    (C) Caleb and Eugene
    (D) Faith and Garth
    (E) Garth and Hannah

41. Which one of the following pairs of swimmers cannot be in the same group as Angus?

    (A) Caleb and Ives
    (B) Eugene and Garth
    (C) Faith and Garth
    (D) Eugene and Hannah
    (E) Garth and Hannah

Example 8

Three types of files—contracts, deeds, and wills—are stored in four sealed drawers. For each of the three types of files, there are exactly three drawers that contain that type. Four tags accurately reflecting the contents of the drawers were created. However, only two of the tags were placed on the correct drawers, and the other two tags were placed on the wrong drawers. As a result, the drawers are tagged as follows:

Drawer 1—Contracts and deeds
Drawer 2—Contracts and wills
Drawer 3—Deeds and wills
Drawer 4—Contracts, deeds and wills

42. If Drawer 3 actually contains no contracts, which one of the following must be true?

    (A) Drawer 1 is correctly tagged.
    (B) Drawer 2 is correctly tagged.
    (C) Drawer 3 is correctly tagged.
    (D) Drawer 1 contains no contracts.
    (E) Drawer 2 contains no deeds.

43. If Drawer 4 actually contains no contracts , which one of the following must be true?

    (A) Drawer 3 is correctly tagged.
    (B) Drawer 4 is correctly tagged.
    (C) Drawer 1 is incorrectly tagged.
    (D) Drawer 2 is incorrectly tagged.
    (E) Drawer 3 is incorrectly tagged.

44. If Drawer 1 is correctly tagged, which one of the following must be true?

    (A) Drawer 2 contains no contracts.
    (B) Drawer 2 contains no deeds.
    (C) Drawer 2 contains no wills.
    (D) Drawer 4 contains some contracts.
    (E) Drawer 4 contains some wills.

45. If Drawer 1 and Drawer 4 are the wrongly tagged drawers, which one the following must be true?

    (A) Drawer 1 contains some files of all three types.
    (B) Drawer 2 contains some files of all three types.
    (C) Drawer 3 contains some files of all three types.
    (D) Drawer 3 contains no deeds.
    (E) Drawer 3 contains no wills.

46. If Drawer 1 and Drawer 4 are the correctly tagged drawers, which one the following must be true?

    (A) Both Drawer 1 and Drawer 2 contain contracts.
    (B) Both Drawer 1 and Drawer 2 contain deeds.
    (C) Both Drawer 1 and Drawer 3 contain deeds.
    (D) Both Drawer 2 and Drawer 3 contain contracts.
    (E) Both Drawer 3 and Drawer 4 contain deeds.

47. If at least contracts and deeds are known to be in Drawer 4, which one of the following must be true?

    (A) If Drawer 1 contains at least contracts and deeds, Drawer 2 contains wills.
    (B) If Drawer 1 contains only contracts and deeds, Drawer 2 contains contracts.
    (C) If Drawer 2 contains only contracts and deeds, Drawer 1 does not contain contracts.
    (D) If Drawer 2 contains at least deeds and wills, Drawer 4 does not contain wills.
    (E) If Drawer 3 contains at least contracts and wills, Drawer 2 does not contain wills.

Example 9

An executive is attending her company's annual convention. The convention features speeches, six of which are to be attended by the executive. The executive must attend two speeches from among three speeches from the research department—B, C, and D; two from among four speeches from the advertising department—F, G, H, and J; and two from among three speeches from the marketing department—P, Q, and R. The following restrictions apply:

If the executive attends G, then she must also attend C.

If the executive attends F, then she will attend neither C nor H.

If the executive attends P, then she will attend neither R nor J.

If the executive attends both C and H, then C is attended some time before H.

P cannot be the fifth speech attended by the executive unless one of the speeches from the advertising department is the first speech attended.

48. Which one of the following is an acceptable sequence of speeches attended by the executive?

	1	2	3	4	5	6
(A)	B	R	F	G	Q	D
(B)	D	C	Q	H	R	G
(C)	D	Q	J	C	R	F
(D)	J	Q	C	B	P	H
(E)	P	G	D	H	C	R

49. If the six speeches to be attended by the executive are C, D, G, H, Q, and R, and if G is to be attended first, then which one of the following speeches CANNOT be attended second?

(A) C
(B) D
(C) H
(D) Q
(E) R

50. If C, H, and Q are the first three speeches to be attended, not necessarily in that order, which one of the following is a speech that CANNOT be attended fifth?

(A) B
(B) D
(C) G
(D) J
(E) P

51. If H is the first speech attended, which one of the following is a speech that must also be attended?

(A) C
(B) D
(C) F
(D) G
(E) P

52. Which one of the following is a speech that must be attended?

(A) C
(B) D
(C) H
(D) Q
(E) R

53. Which one of the following is a speech that CANNOT be attended if G is attended?

(A) F
(B) H
(C) J
(D) P
(E) R

Example 10

Six coffees—A, B, C, D, E, and F—are being judged and ranked in terms of taste. The coffees can be ranked, from best to worst, Superior, Very Good, Good, Fair, and Poor, and coffees can have the same rank as each other. Ranks are considered consecutive if they are next to each other; for example, Superior and Very Good are consecutive, and Superior and Good are not. Any coffee that receives the rank of Poor is disqualified.

The ranks of B and E are consecutive.
The ranks of D and F are consecutive.
The rank of A is higher than that of C.
The rank of B is higher than that of E.

54. If A and D have the same rank, and if F is disqualified, which one of the following must be true?

    (A) B is ranked Very Good.
    (B) C is ranked Fair.
    (C) C is ranked Poor.
    (D) E is ranked Very Good.
    (E) E is ranked Good.

55. If none of the coffees is disqualified, and B receives a higher rank than either D or F, which one of the following must be true?

    (A) Exactly one coffee is ranked Superior.
    (B) Exactly one coffee is ranked Very Good.
    (C) Exactly two coffees are ranked Very Good.
    (D) At least one coffee is ranked Very Good and at least one coffee is ranked Good.
    (E) At least one coffee is ranked Good and at least one coffee is ranked Fair.

56. If E ranks higher than A and A ranks higher than either D or F, which one of the following allows all six of the coffees' ranks to be determined?

    (A) C ranks Fair.
    (B) D ranks Fair.
    (C) C and D have the same rank.
    (D) C and F have the same rank.
    (E) C ranks higher than F.

57. If E ranks higher than A, and C ranks higher than D, exactly how many of the coffees' ranks can be determined?

    (A) 2
    (B) 3
    (C) 4
    (D) 5
    (E) 6

58. Assume E ranks higher than D and is consecutive with it, and that the ranks of F and E differ. Which one of the following must be true?

    (A) There is a coffee ranked Superior and a coffee ranked Very Good.
    (B) There is a coffee ranked Superior and a coffee ranked Good.
    (C) There is a coffee ranked Very Good and a coffee ranked Fair.
    (D) There is a coffee ranked Very Good and a coffee ranked Poor.
    (E) There is a coffee ranked Fair and a coffee ranked Poor.

59. Assume that A ranks lower than E. At least one coffee must have been disqualified if which one of the following is also true?

    (A) D ranks lower than A.
    (B) D ranks lower than E.
    (C) E ranks lower than D.
    (D) F ranks lower than A.
    (E) F ranks lower than C.

LEVEL 3

The games in this section have the same level of difficulty as difficult LSAT games. Enter at your own risk. Ask yourself if you should really be here, according to the way you score. But if you like a challenge, remember:

Step 1: Decide on the appropriate diagram and draw it.

Step 2: Symbolize the clues.

Step 3: Double-check your work and make deductions.

Step 4: Decide question order (not for GRE CAT).

Step 5: Keep your pencil moving.

Example 1

From exactly seven books—D, E, F, G, H, I, J—exactly four books are being purchased, in accordance with the following conditions:

If D is purchased, F must also be purchased.
If E is purchased, G must also be purchased.
If H and I are both purchased, F cannot be purchased.

1. If H and I are both purchased, which one of the following must also be purchased?

   (A) D
   (B) E
   (C) F
   (D) G
   (E) J

2. If E and J are both purchased, each of the following could also be purchased EXCEPT

   (A) D
   (B) F
   (C) G
   (D) H
   (E) I

3. If G is not purchased, which one of the following can be, but does not have to be, purchased?

   (A) D
   (B) E
   (C) F
   (D) H
   (E) J

Example 2

A certain music store sells musical recordings only in vinyl, compact disc, and tape formats, and only in folk, jazz, and rock genres. Travis purchases exactly three recordings from the store.

    Travis does not purchase two recordings that have the same format and genre.

    Travis does not purchase both a vinyl recording and a tape recording.

    There are no vinyl folk recordings.

    There are no tape rock recordings.

4.   Which one of the following must be false?

   (A) Two of the recordings that Travis purchases are vinyl and two are folk.

   (B) Two of the recordings that Travis purchases are compact disc and two are folk.

   (C) Two of the recordings that Travis purchases are tape and two are folk.

   (D) Two of the recordings that Travis purchases are vinyl, one is jazz, and one is rock.

   (E) Two of the recordings that Travis purchases are compact disc, one is jazz, and one is rock.

5.   If Travis purchases a vinyl rock recording, which one of the following must be false?

   (A) Travis purchases two rock recordings.

   (B) Travis purchases two folk recordings.

   (C) Travis purchases two jazz recordings.

   (D) Travis purchases two vinyl recordings.

   (E) Travis purchases two compact disc recordings.

6.   If Travis does not purchase a compact disc jazz recording, which one of the following must be true?

   (A) Travis purchases either a compact disc folk recording or a vinyl rock recording.

   (B) Travis purchases either a compact disc folk recording or a compact disc rock recording.

   (C) Travis purchases either a tape folk recording or a vinyl rock recording.

   (D) Travis purchases either a tape folk recording or a compact disc folk recording

   (E) Travis purchases either a tape jazz recording or a vinyl jazz recording.

7.   If Travis purchases exactly one compact disc recording and does not purchase two recordings of the same genre, then he cannot purchase which one of the following?

   (A) a compact disc folk recording

   (B) a compact disc jazz recording

   (C) a compact disc rock recording

   (D) a tape folk recording

   (E) a tape jazz recording

8.   If neither a tape folk recording nor a vinyl rock recording is available, which one of the following must Travis purchase?

   (A) a folk recording

   (B) a compact disc jazz recording

   (C) either a tape recording or a vinyl recording

   (D) either a compact disc folk recording or a compact disc rock recording

   (E) either a tape jazz recording or a compact disc rock recording

Example 3

Each of seven guests at a barbecue chooses one of two types of meals—a hot meal or a cold meal. Each guest is either a child, a man, or a woman. Two of the guests are children, two are men, and three are women. The following is known about the meals the guests choose:

> If the two children and at least one of the women choose the same type of meal as each other, then both men also choose that type of meal.
>
> If the three women choose the same type of meal as each other, then no child chooses that type of meal.
>
> At least two of the guests choose a hot meal, and at least two choose a cold meal at the barbecue.
>
> At least one child chooses a cold meal.

9. If the two men do not choose the same type of meal as each other, then which one of the following could be true?

   (A) No child and exactly two women choose a hot meal.
   (B) Exactly one child and exactly one woman choose a hot meal.
   (C) Exactly one child and all three women choose a hot meal.
   (D) Exactly two children and exactly one woman choose a hot meal.
   (E) Exactly two children and exactly two women choose a hot meal.

10. Which one of the following must be true?

    (A) At least one child chooses a hot meal.
    (B) At least one woman does not choose a hot meal.
    (C) At least one woman chooses a hot meal.
    (D) At least one man does not choose a hot meal.
    (E) At least one man chooses a hot meal.

11. If the three women all choose the same type of meal, which one of the following must be true?

    (A) Both men choose a hot meal.
    (B) Both men choose a cold meal.
    (C) One child chooses a hot meal and one child does not choose a hot meal.
    (D) One man chooses a hot meal and one man does not choose a hot meal.
    (E) All three women choose a hot meal.

12. If exactly two guests choose a cold meal, then which one of the following must be true?

    (A) Both men choose a hot meal.
    (B) Exactly one child chooses a hot meal.
    (C) No child chooses a hot meal.
    (D) Exactly two women choose a hot meal.
    (E) Exactly three women choose a hot meal.

13. Each of the following could be a complete and accurate list of those guests who choose a hot meal at the barbecue EXCEPT

    (A) two women
    (B) one child, one woman
    (C) two men, three women
    (D) one child, two men, two women
    (E) one child, two men, three women

14. If the two children choose the same type of meal, but the women do not all choose hot meals, then each of the following must be true EXCEPT:

    (A) Both children choose a cold meal.
    (B) Both men choose a hot meal.
    (C) At least one woman does not choose a hot meal.
    (D) Exactly two women choose a hot meal.
    (E) Exactly five of the guests choose a cold meal.

Example 4

A game involves ten children, five "throwers" and five "catchers" each on different teams, as follows:

Team	Throwers	Catchers
Red	A	B, C
Yellow	D	E
Purple	F, G, H	J, K

The game is played by pairs of children consisting of one thrower and one catcher of the same color. At most, two pairs can be on the field at a time; the remaining children must be in two rows on the side of the field. The game is bound by the following conditions:

Neither row can include more than four children.

Any two children that are both of the same position and of the same team as each other cannot be in a row together.

Whenever either B or K is on the field, H cannot be on the field.

15. Which one of the following is a possible assignment of the children?

	Row	Row	Field
(A)	A, D, E	B, C, H	F, G, J, K
(B)	C, D, F	E, G, K	A, B, H, J
(C)	C, F, H	G, J, K	A, B, D, E
(D)	A, B, D, G	C, E, H, K	F, J
(E)	A, B, D, G, K	C, E, H	F, J, K

16. Which one of the following lists two pairs of children who can be on the field at the same time?

(A) A and B; D and E
(B) A and B; H and J
(C) A and C; D and E
(D) A and C; G and K
(E) D and E; H and K

17. If F and G are among the children that are assigned to the rows, then it must be true that

(A) A is on the field.
(B) C is on the field.
(C) E is on the field.
(D) B is assigned to one of the rows.
(E) J is assigned to one of the rows.

18. If F and J are among the children that are assigned to the rows, which one of the following is a pair of children that must be on the field?

(A) A and B
(B) A and C
(C) D and E
(D) G and K
(E) H and K

19. Which one of the following CANNOT be true?

(A) One pair of children from the Purple team are the only children on the field together.
(B) One pair of children from the Red team and one pair of children from the Yellow team are on the field together.
(C) One pair of children from the Red team and one pair of children from the Purple team are on the field together.
(D) One pair of children from the Yellow team and one pair of children from the Purple team are on the field together.
(E) Two pairs of children from the Purple team are on the field together.

20. If H is one of the children on the field, it must be true that

(A) A is on the field.
(B) D is on the field.
(C) C is assigned to a row.
(D) E is assigned to a row.
(E) G is assigned to a row.

Example 5

Five musicians, and no one else, are competing in a musical competition. The five musicians are ranked from first to fifth, A being the highest rank. The initial order is:

A	B	C	D	E
Fiona	Gilda	Hazel	Justine	Kendra

In the competition, the musicians will compete in cycles alternating between Red cycles and Yellow cycles, though not necessarily in that order.

In a Red cycle, the following ranked musicians will challenge each other: A vs. B; C vs. D.

In a Yellow cycle, the following ranked musicians will challenge each other: B vs. C; D vs. E.

When two players compete, the winner is awarded the higher of the two positions, and the loser is awarded the lower of the two positions.

21. Which one of the following could be the musicians' order after one cycle of challenges?

	A	B	C	D	E
(A)	Fiona	Hazel	Kendra	Gilda	Justine
(B)	Gilda	Fiona	Hazel	Kendra	Justine
(C)	Hazel	Fiona	Gilda	Justine	Kendra
(D)	Fiona	Gilda	Justine	Hazel	Kendra
(E)	Fiona	Gilda	Kendra	Justine	Hazel

22. If Kendra wins matches in each of the first two cycles, how many of the musicians' positions after these two cycles can be definitely determined?

(A) 0
(B) 1
(C) 2
(D) 3
(E) 5

23. If Justine wins at least her first challenge, all of the following could be in position C after the second cycle EXCEPT

(A) Fiona
(B) Gilda
(C) Hazel
(D) Justine
(E) Kendra

24. If, after the completion of two cycles, Fiona has lost her only challenge, which one of the following could be true?

(A) The first cycle was a Red cycle.
(B) Hazel is ranked lower than both Justine and Kendra.
(C) Fiona is ranked third.
(D) Justine is ranked higher than Fiona.
(E) Hazel is ranked higher than Fiona.

25. Which one of the following must be false?

(A) Fiona loses challenges in each of the first two cycles.
(B) Gilda wins challenges in each of the first two cycles.
(C) Gilda loses challenges in each of the first two cycles.
(D) Kendra wins challenges in each of the first two cycles.
(E) Kendra loses challenges in each of the first two cycles.

26. If the order after the third cycle is:

A	B	C	D	E
Hazel	Gilda	Kendra	Fiona	Justine

Which one of the following could have been the order at the completion of the first cycle?

	A	B	C	D	E
(A)	Fiona	Kendra	Hazel	Gilda	Justine
(B)	Gilda	Hazel	Fiona	Kendra	Justine
(C)	Hazel	Fiona	Gilda	Justine	Kendra
(D)	Gilda	Fiona	Hazel	Justine	Kendra
(E)	Fiona	Gilda	Kendra	Justine	Hazel

5

Example 6

A certain board game involves six pieces—U, V, W, X, Y, and Z. They are initially set up on the board as follows:

Row 1:   U   V   W

Row 2:   X   Y   Z

The game involves the pieces switching positions. The four possible switches—two of them turns and two of them moves—are described below. No other pieces besides the pieces referred to in the descriptions of the switches below ever change positions.

Turns:

There is a purple turn (PT), in which U switches to the place formerly occupied by V; V switches to the place formerly occupied by W; and W switches to the place formerly occupied by U.

There is an orange turn (OT), in which each U and W switch to the places formerly occupied by the other.

Moves:

There is a blue move (BM), in which the pieces in Row 2 switch places so as to be opposite those pieces in Row 1 that they faced at the beginning of the game.

There is a gray move (GM), in which the pieces in Row 1 switch so as to be opposite those pieces in Row 2 that they faced at the beginning of the game.

Two consecutive turns cannot be followed by a third turn.

If, during the game, the pieces end up in their original positions, the next switch cannot be a move.

27. If the first switch in the game is OT, followed by BM, which one of the following represents the positions of the pieces after those two switches?

(A) U   V   W
    X   Y   Z

(B) V   U   W
    X   Y   Z

(C) W   V   U
    Z   Y   X

(D) U   W   V
    X   Y   Z

(E) W   U   V
    X   Y   Z

28. If the pieces' positions are: V   U   W
                                    Y   X   Z

which one of the following sequences of pieces in Row 1 is possible after exactly one other switch?

(A) U V W
(B) V U W
(C) V W U
(D) W U V
(E) W V U

29. If the game started with the pieces in their original positions, and the pieces have switched exactly two times, both of them turns, which one of the following could be the resulting positions of the pieces?

(A) W U V
    X Y Z
(B) U W V
    X Z Y
(C) W V U
    X Z Y
(D) U W V
    X Y Z
(E) W V U
    Z Y X

30. Starting from the original position, which one of the following switches or sequences of switches will result in the following positions for the pieces:

    V   U   W?
    Y   X   Z

(A) OT
(B) PT
(C) OT, PT
(D) PT, BM
(E) OT, PT, BM

31. If the game begins with PT followed by BM, which one of the following switches or sequences of switches will result in the pieces returning to their original positions?

(A) OT
(B) PT
(C) PT, PT
(D) OT, BM
(E) PT, PT, BM

Example 7

Rick, an artist, uses four special paint colors—yellow, magenta, cyan, and black—that he keeps, respectively, in exactly four buckets—P, Q, R, and S. Each bucket originally contains one color, and Rick is mixing these paints together. A "mix" consists of mixing exactly two of these paints together by completely emptying the contents of one of the buckets into another of the buckets. The following restrictions apply:
   The product of a mix cannot be used in further mixes.
   Mixing the contents of P and Q produces a yellow paint.
   Mixing the contents of Q and R produces a black paint.
   Mixing the contents of R with the contents of either P or
      S produces a magenta paint.
   Mixing the contents of S with the contents of either P or
      Q produces a cyan paint.

32. If Rick creates exactly one mix, which one of the following could be the colors of the paints in the resulting three buckets?

   (A) magenta, magenta, cyan
   (B) magenta, black, black
   (C) magenta, black, yellow
   (D) cyan, cyan, yellow
   (E) cyan, black, black

33. If Rick creates exactly two mixes, which one of the following could be the colors of the paints in the resulting two buckets?

   (A) magenta, magenta
   (B) magenta, black
   (C) magenta, yellow
   (D) cyan, yellow
   (E) black, black

34. If Rick creates exactly one mix and none of the resulting three buckets contains a yellow paint, which one of the following could be the colors of the paints in the three buckets?

   (A) magenta, magenta, cyan
   (B) magenta, cyan, cyan
   (C) magenta, cyan, black
   (D) magenta, black, black
   (E) cyan, cyan, black

35. If Rick creates exactly one mix and exactly one of the resulting three buckets contains a magenta paint, which of the following could be colors in the other two buckets?

   (A) both cyan
   (B) both black
   (C) both yellow
   (D) one cyan and one yellow
   (E) one black and one yellow

36. If Rick creates exactly two mixes and after the first mix exactly one of the resulting three buckets contains a black paint, then in the second mix Rick could mix together the contents of buckets

   (A) P and Q
   (B) P and R
   (C) P and S
   (D) Q and R
   (E) R and S

37. If Rick creates exactly one mix and none of the resulting three buckets contains a black paint, then Rick must have mixed the contents of

   (A) bucket P with bucket Q
   (B) bucket P with bucket S
   (C) bucket Q with bucket S
   (D) bucket Q with one of the other buckets
   (E) bucket S with one of the other buckets

38. If Rick creates exactly two mixes and exactly one of the resulting two buckets contains a black paint, then it must be true that the contents of the other resulting bucket is

   (A) obtained by mixing buckets P and Q
   (B) obtained by mixing buckets Q and S
   (C) magenta
   (D) cyan
   (E) yellow

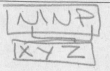

Handwritten: Red MNP — 1st / White XYZ — 2nd

Example 8

A vintner makes six wines. M, N, and P are reds. X, Y, and Z are whites.

The vintner always bottles and labels the reds first. Within their respective groups, the vintner bottles those wines that she makes comparatively more of before she bottles those wines that she makes comparatively fewer of.

The vintner labels her wines, in their respective groups, in the opposite order of their bottling.

She bottles more of P than of X, and there is no wine that she bottles both more than X and less than P.

She bottles more of Y than of N, and there is no wine that she bottles both less than Y and more than N.

She bottles the same amount of Z as she does of M.

39. If M is bottled first and P third, which one of the following must be true?

    (A) Z is bottled fifth.
    (B) Z is bottled last.
    (C) X is bottled fifth.
    (D) X is bottled last.
    (E) Y is bottled fourth.

40. If P is labeled first, which one of the following could NOT be possible?

    (A) M is bottled before P.
    (B) N is bottled before M.
    (C) X is bottled before Z.
    (D) Y is bottled after Z.
    (E) Z is bottled before X.

41. Which one of the following is NOT a possible labeling order?

    (A) M, P, N, Z, X, Y
    (B) N, M, P, Y, Z, X
    (C) N, P, M, Y, X, Z
    (D) P, M, N, X, Z, Y
    (E) P, N, M, Z, Y, X

42. Suppose the vintner bottles the reds after the whites on a day she labels Y fourth and P second. The order of bottling must be

    (A) X, Y, Z, P, N, M
    (B) X, Z, Y, P, M, N
    (C) Z, X, Y, M, P, N
    (D) Z, Y, X, M, N, P
    (E) Y, X, Z, N, P, M

43. Suppose the vintner does not label the reds first, but alternates by labeling a white, then a red. If N is bottled first, it would NOT be possible for which pair of wines to be labeled sequentially?

    (A) M immediately before X
    (B) X immediately before P
    (C) P immediately before Z
    (D) Y immediately before N
    (E) Z immediately before Y

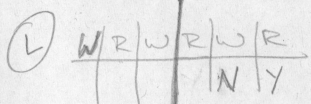

Example 9

Exactly six watches—B, C, E, F, H, and J—are being displayed in a row in a jeweler's window. The left-most watch is first, and the right-most watch is sixth. The first, second, third, and fourth watches are all displayed on velvet cushions. The following conditions apply to the display of the watches:

Each watch is either gold or silver, but not both.
Two of the six watches have leather bands and four have metal bands.
Both leather-banded watches, exactly one of which is silver, are displayed on velvet cushions.
Exactly one silver watch is displayed on a velvet cushion.
Watches B and E are displayed to the left of watch F, and watch F is displayed to the left of watches C and H.
Watches B and E are gold.
Watches F and J are silver.

44. Which one of the following is a complete and accurate list of the watches that can be gold?

    (A) B, C
    (B) B, E
    (C) B, C, E
    (D) B, E, H
    (E) B, C, E, H

45. Which one of the following statements CANNOT be true?

    (A) A gold watch with a leather band is displayed second.
    (B) A silver watch with a leather band is displayed second.
    (C) A silver watch with a leather band is displayed third.
    (D) A gold watch with a metal band is displayed fourth.
    (E) A gold watch with a leather band is displayed fourth.

46. Which one of the following watches must have a metal band?

    (A) watch B
    (B) watch E
    (C) watch F
    (D) watch H
    (E) watch J

47. Which one of the following statements can be false?

    (A) Watch B is displayed to the left of watch E.
    (B) Watch B is displayed to the left of watch H.
    (C) Watch E is displayed to the left of watch J.
    (D) Watch E is displayed to the left of watch H.
    (E) Watch F is displayed to the left of watch J.

48. If watch C has a leather band, which one of the following statements can be false?

    (A) Watch B has a metal band.
    (B) Watch E has a metal band.
    (C) Watch C is displayed fourth.
    (D) Watch C is gold.
    (E) Watch H is gold.

49. If watch H is displayed fourth, then which one of the following statements must be true?

    (A) Watch B has a metal band.
    (B) Watch C has a metal band.
    (C) Watch H has a metal band.
    (D) Watch C is silver.
    (E) Watch H is silver.

50. Which one of the following statements could be true?

    (A) Watch B is not displayed on a velvet cushion.
    (B) Watch E is not displayed on a velvet cushion.
    (C) Watch F is not displayed on a velvet cushion.
    (D) Watch H is displayed on a velvet cushion.
    (E) Watch J is displayed on a velvet cushion.

Example 10

The psychology department at a major university has been asked to publish a report on a recent experiment, and a committee is being formed to carry out that request. The committee will have five members—L, M, N, P, and Q. Each committee member holds exactly one of the following positions: faculty advisor, graduate student, or undergraduate student. Only the faculty advisor is not advised. Other committee members are each advised by exactly one committee member, who is either a faculty advisor or a graduate student. Each advised committee member holds a different position than his or her advisor. The following conditions apply:

There is exactly one faculty advisor.

At least one of the committee members whom the faculty advisor advises is a graduate student.

Each graduate student advises at least one committee member.

L does not advise any committee member.

M advises exactly two committee members.

51. Which one of the following is an acceptable assignment of committee members to the positions?

	Faculty Advisor	Graduate Student	Undergraduate Student
(A)	M	N, P, Q	L
(B)	M	N	L, P, Q
(C)	N	L, M	P, Q
(D)	N, P	M	L, Q
(E)	P	L, M, N, Q	—

52. Which one of the following must be true?

(A) There are at most three undergraduate students.
(B) There is exactly one undergraduate student.
(C) There are at least two graduate students.
(D) There are exactly two graduate students.
(E) There are exactly two committee members who advise no one.

53. Which one of the following is a pair of committee members who could both be graduate students?

(A) L, N
(B) L, Q
(C) M, P
(D) M, Q
(E) P, Q

54. Which one of the following could be true?

(A) There is exactly one undergraduate student.
(B) There are exactly two graduate students.
(C) There are exactly two committee members who are not advised.
(D) There are more graduate students than undergraduate students.
(E) The faculty advisor advises all of the other committee members.

55. If L is advised by the faculty advisor, which one of the following must be true?

(A) M is the faculty advisor.
(B) N is the faculty advisor.
(C) Q is an undergraduate student.
(D) There is exactly one graduate student.
(E) There are exactly two undergraduate students.

56. If P advises exactly two committee members, which one of the following must be true?

(A) L is advised by P.
(B) M is a graduate student.
(C) Q is advised.
(D) There are exactly two graduate students.
(E) There are exactly two undergraduate students.

CHAPTER

6

Answers and Explanations

READ THESE!

So, you're a games whiz and you got all the answers right. Read the explanations anyway. On the chance that you guessed on one or two answers, or even missed a few, the explanations will clarify what you did right or what you did wrong. If you already know this stuff, the explanations will reinforce your knowledge. If you're not a games whiz yet, read these explanations, and you'll be closer to becoming one.

By the way, these explanations are written with the assumption that you did the "If" questions first.

ANSWER KEY, LEVEL 1

Example 1
1. A
2. A
3. B
4. E

Example 2
5. D
6. C
7. A
8. B
9. E

Example 3
10. A
11. C
12. D
13. B
14. B

Example 4
15. E
16. A
17. B
18. A
19. E

Example 5
20. D
21. B
22. C
23. A
24. D
25. A

Example 6
26. D
27. B
28. C
29. B
30. A
31. E

Example 7
32. D
33. E
34. A
35. E
36. C
37. D

Example 8
38. D
39. A
40. E
41. D

Example 9
42. E
43. A
44. D
45. D
46. B
47. A

Example 10
48. C
49. A
50. C
51. B
52. D
53. B
54. C

EXPLANATIONS, LEVEL 1

Example 1

A jeweler is preparing a window display of gems. There is a left display case and a right display case. In each display case, the jeweler will show three of seven of gems—an amethyst, a diamond, an emerald, a garnet, an opal, a ruby and a sapphire. The gems must be shown according to the following restrictions:

The amethyst must be included in the window and it must be shown in the left display case.

The diamond must be included in the window and it must be shown in the right display case.

The ruby can neither be shown in the same display case as the diamond nor in the same display case as the garnet.

The emerald and the sapphire must be included in the window and must be shown together in one display case.

Here's the diagram:

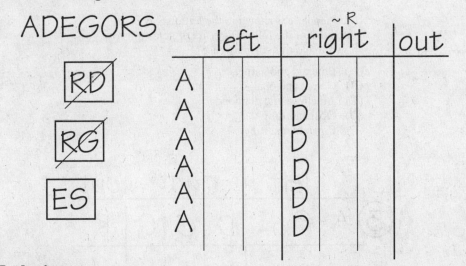

TYPE: Assignment

Notice that "not R" deduction over the "right" column. We got that from that RD antiblock. Also, because not every gem will be displayed, we need an "out" column.

1. Which one of the following combinations of gems can be shown in the left display case?

   (A) Amethyst, opal, ruby
   (B) Amethyst, emerald, opal
   (C) Amethyst, garnet, sapphire
   (D) Amethyst, diamond, ruby
   (E) Diamond, emerald, sapphire

Check your clues and systematically eliminate choices. We already know that the amethyst is in the left case, so eliminate (E). We also know that the diamond is in the right case, so eliminate (D). We know that the emerald and the sapphire are a block, so eliminate (B) and (C). That leaves us with the answer, (A).

2. Which one of the following combinations of gems can be shown in the right display case?

    (A) Diamond, garnet, opal
    (B) Diamond, garnet, ruby
    (C) Diamond, ruby, sapphire
    (D) Amethyst, diamond, opal
    (E) Diamond, emerald, garnet

Check your clues and systematically eliminate choices. We already know that the amethyst is in the left case, so eliminate (D). We know that the emerald and the sapphire are a block, so eliminate (C) and (E). We know that the ruby and the garnet can't be together (that's an antiblock), and also that the ruby and diamond can't be together (RD antiblock), so eliminate (B). That leaves us with the answer, (A).

3. If the sapphire is shown in the left display case, which one of the following pairs of gems must be shown in the right display case?

    (A) Emerald and garnet
    (B) Garnet and opal
    (C) Amethyst and diamond
    (D) Opal and ruby
    (E) Emerald and ruby

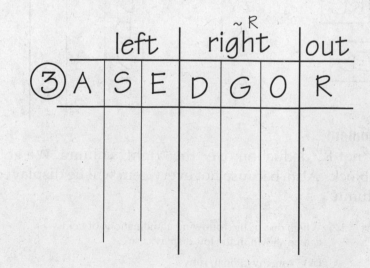

Since we have an ES block, the left display case contains ASE. Eliminate (A), (C), and (E). Since the ruby can never be in the right display case, because it can't be with the diamond, eliminate (D). So, our answer is (B).

4. If the sapphire is shown in the right display case, which one of the following pairs of gems could be shown in the left display case?

(A) Emerald and garnet
(B) Emerald and opal
(C) Emerald and ruby
(D) Garnet and ruby
(E) Opal and ruby

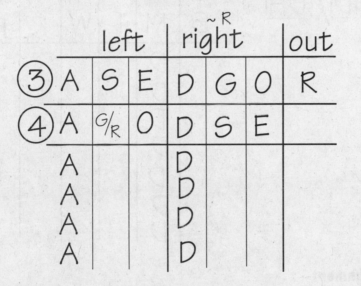

Since we have an ES block, the right display case contains DSE. Eliminate (A), (B), and (C). Since the ruby can never be with the garnet (antiblock), eliminate (D). So, our answer is (E). This COULD be true.

Example 2

A student must see seven films for a film studies class, one film on each night of a certain week, Sunday through Saturday. The possible films are B, C, D, E, F, G, and H. The following conditions must be met when determining the student's schedule:
  B must be seen on either the night before or the night after F is seen.
  C must be seen on either the night before or the night after either E or G is seen.
  H cannot be seen on the night before or on the night after D is seen.
  D must be seen on Monday.

Here's the diagram:

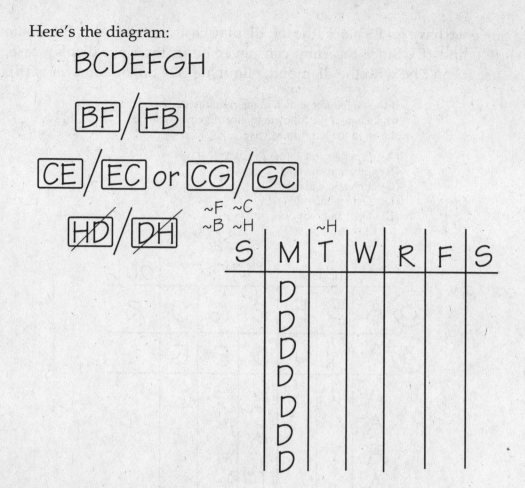

TYPE: Assignment

Notice those "not H" deductions over Sunday and Tuesday. We got that from that HD/DH antiblock. Also, because C has to be before or after E or G, it can't be on Sunday, because we already know D is on Monday. Same with B and F. They are in a block, so neither can go on Sunday

5. Which one of the following is a possible film schedule for the student, in order from Sunday to Saturday?

    (A) B, F, C, G, H, E, D
    (B) C, E, B, F, D, G, H
    (C) F, D, B, H, E, C, G
    (D) **G, D, C, E, H, B, F**
    (E) G, D, H, E, C, B, F

Take each clue and systematically apply it to the answer choices. The easiest one is D on Monday. That eliminates choices (A) and (B). The BF/FB block eliminates choice (C). The DH antiblock eliminates choice (E). That leaves us with the correct answer, (D).

6. If B is seen on Saturday, which one of the following must be true?

(A) F is seen on Thursday.
(B) C is seen on Tuesday.
(C) H is seen on Thursday.
(D) E is seen on Wednesday.
(E) G is seen on Sunday.

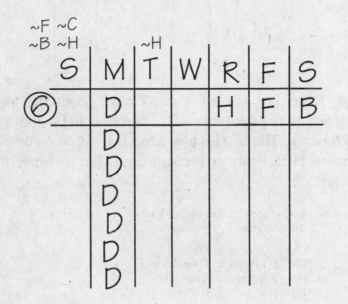

B on Saturday puts F on Friday, because of the BF/FB block. H is our next most restricted element, and since it can't be on Sunday or Tuesday, that leaves Wednesday or Thursday. Putting it on Wednesday wouldn't leave any room for any of the C blocks, so it goes on Thursday. So, the answer is (C).

7. If G is seen on Thursday, E must be seen on

(A) Sunday
(B) Tuesday
(C) Wednesday
(D) Friday
(E) Saturday

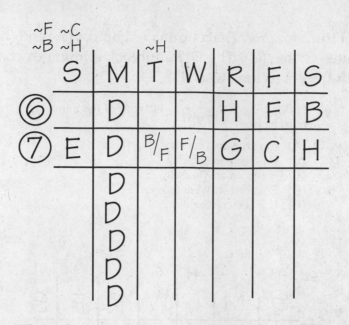

With G on Thursday, we must think next about the location of our blocks, as well as the restrictions on H. There has to be room for a C block and the BF/FB block. The BF/FB block can only go on Tuesday/Wednesday, which means H can only go on Saturday. That forces E on Sunday. So, the answer is (A).

8. If C is seen on Saturday, which one of the following must be true?

   (A) G is seen on Friday.
   (B) H is seen on Thursday.
   (C) F is seen on Wednesday.
   (D) B is seen on Tuesday.
   (E) E is seen on Sunday.

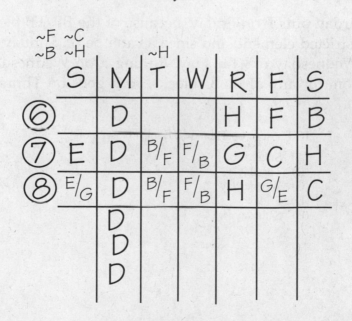

C is attached to blocks. So C on Saturday means either E or G is on Friday. H is our next most restricted element, and since it can't be on Sunday or Tuesday, that leaves Wednesday or Thursday. Putting it on Wednesday wouldn't leave any room for the BF/FB block, so it goes on Thursday. The answer is (B).

9. Which one of the following is a night on which H could be seen?

   (A) Sunday
   (B) Tuesday
   (C) Wednesday
   (D) Friday
   (E) Saturday

Use your past setups for this one. Check out the diagram for the last question. We've gotten H to be on Thursday and Saturday. Thursday's not a choice, but Saturday is. So, the answer is (E). See how important it is to not erase your work?

Example 3

A communications system involves sending electronic mail to exactly four computer terminals: F, G, H, and J. Electronic mail travels from one computer terminal directly to another computer terminal only as follows:

From F to G
From F to H
From F to J
From J to F
From G to H
From H to G
From G to J
From J to H

A single direct path going in one direction from one computer terminal to another is referred to as a pathway.

Here's the diagram:

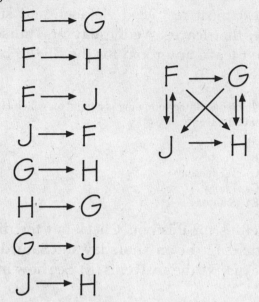

F —→ G

F —→ H

F —→ J

J —→ F

G —→ H

H —→ G

G —→ J

J —→ H

TYPE: Non-Assignment, Path/Map

Symbolize each connection separately, then put them together any way you want. Your diagram might have looked slightly different from this one, but that's okay. Make the connections any way you want, just as long as the *right* connections are made. Also, don't mistake these arrows for "if-then" arrows. These are just regular directional arrows. Notice that some arrows only point in one direction, while others point in both directions. Remember, the nice thing about a game like this is that once you draw the diagram, you never have to touch it again.

10. If a piece of electronic mail is to travel from H to G over as few pathways as possible, it must travel in which one of the following ways?

   (A) Directly from H to G
   (B) Via F but no other computer terminal
   (C) Via J but no other computer terminal
   (D) Via F and J, in that order
   (E) Via J and F, in that order

Isn't there a direct path from H to G? Yep. So, the answer is (A).

11. Which one of the following is a complete and accurate list of computer terminals to which a piece of electronic mail can be sent along exactly one pathway from J?

   (A) F
   (B) H
   (C) F, H
   (D) G, H
   (E) F, G, H

What is J directly connected to? F and H, so the answer is (C).

12. Which one of the following sequences of pathways is a path over which a piece of electronic mail could travel from G back to G?

    (A) From G to F, from F to G
    (B) From G to H, from H to F, from F to J, from J to G
    (C) From G to II, from H to J, from J to F, from F to G
    (D) From G to J, from J to F, from F to H, from H to G
    (E) From G to J, from J to H, from H to F, from F to G

Let's try 'em. In (A), we're supposed to go from G to F, but that path doesn't exist, so eliminate (A). In (B), we're supposed to go from H to F, but that path doesn't exist, so eliminate (B). In (C), we're supposed to go from H to J, but that path doesn't exist, so eliminate (C). In (D), we can go from G to J to F to H and back to G, so that's it!

13. If all of the pathways in the system are equal in length, and if messages always travel along the shortest possible path, then the longest path any piece of electronic mail travels in the system is the path from

    (A) G to F
    (B) H to F
    (C) H to J
    (D) J to F
    (E) J to G

Let's try 'em. In (A), the path is G-J-F. In (B), the path is H-G-J-F. In (C), the path is H-G-J. In (D), the path is J-F. In (E), the path is J-F-G. The longest path is the one in (B).

14. If certain restricted pieces of electronic mail are allowed to travel from one terminal to another only if travel can be completed by using a single pathway, and if an addition of one pathway is to be made to the system so that such restricted pieces of electronic mail can be sent from each computer terminal to at least two others and also be received by each computer terminal from at least two others, then that addition must be from

    (A) G to F
    (B) H to F
    (C) H to J
    (D) J to F
    (E) J to G

What is this question asking? It's asking "which path should be added so that each terminal sends and receives from two terminals?" So let's figure out which terminal doesn't already do that and add a pathway there. F sends to 2 (G and H) only receives from 1 (G). H receives from 3 (G, F, and J) but only sends to one (G). So add a pathway from H to F, so that H and F both send to and receive from at least 2 terminals. That's (B).

Example 4

An artist has exactly seven paintings—T, U, V, W, X, Y, and Z—from which she must choose exactly five to be in an exhibit. Any combination is acceptable provided it meets the following conditions:
  If T is chosen, X cannot be chosen.
  If U is chosen, Y must also be chosen.
  If V is chosen, X must also be chosen.

Here's the diagram:

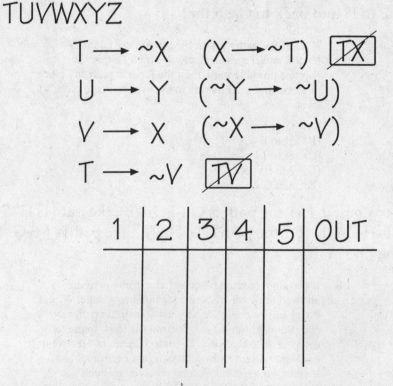

TYPE: Assignment

Since not every painting gets chosen, this diagram has an "out" column. The cool thing about it is that if you get two paintings in the "out" column," you automatically know that all other paintings are "in." Notice the contrapositives in parentheses next to each clue. (Remember, REVERSE AND NEGATE.) Also take note of the TX antiblock deduction. Remember, in an "if-then" situation, if one is in and one is out, it's an antiblock. We got that TV antiblock by linking the TX antiblock with "if V then X."

15. Which one of the following is an acceptable combination of paintings for inclusion in the exhibit?

(A) T, U, V, X, Y
(B) T, U, V, Y, Z
(C) T, W, X, Y, Z
(D) U, V, W, Y, Z
(E) U, V, W, X, Y

Check your clues and systematically eliminate choices that violate them. First, the TX antiblock eliminates (A) and (C). Next, "if V then X" eliminates (B) and (D). That leaves us with (E), the answer.

16. If the artist chooses painting V to be included among the paintings in the exhibit, which one of the following must be true of that combination of paintings?

(A) T is not chosen.
(B) Y is not chosen.
(C) U is chosen.
(D) W is chosen.
(E) Z is chosen.

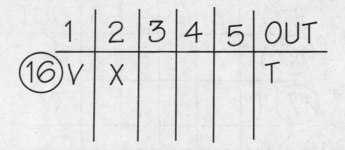

V is in, which means X is in, which means T is out. That's all we know for sure. The answer is (A).

17. If painting T is chosen to be among the paintings included in the exhibit, which one of the following cannot be chosen to be among the paintings in the exhibit?

(A) U
(B) V
(C) W
(D) Y
(E) Z

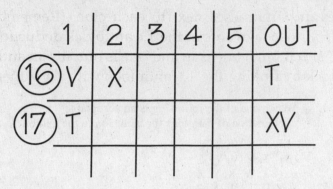

	1	2	3	4	5	OUT
⑯	V	X				T
⑰	T					XV

T is in, which means X is out. If X is out, then V is out (remember, that's the contrapositive of "if V then X"). That's all we know for sure. The answer is (B).

18.   If the artist does not choose painting Z for the exhibit, which one of the following also cannot be chosen?

(A) T
(B) U
(C) V
(D) W
(E) X

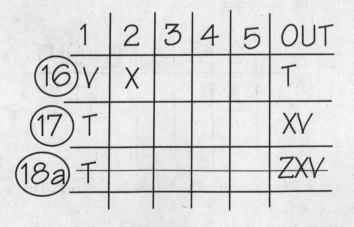

	1	2	3	4	5	OUT
⑯	V	X				T
⑰	T					XV
⑱a	~~T~~					~~ZXV~~

Z is out. This doesn't tell us much. So, let's try the answers. To try (A), try choosing T. If T is in, then means X is out. If X is out, then V is out (remember, that's the contrapositive of "if V then X"). But we can't have three paintings out, because we have to choose five out of seven. So, since this setup doesn't work, T cannot be chosen, and the answer is (A). Don't forget to draw a line through that setup, so you don't use it by mistake later; you only want to keep correct arrangements.

> 19. Which one of the following substitutions can the artist always make without violating the restrictions affecting the combination of paintings, given that the painting mentioned first was not, and the painting mentioned second was, originally going to be chosen?
>
> (A) T substitutes for V.
> (B) U substitutes for Y.
> (C) V substitutes for X.
> (D) W substitutes for Y.
> (E) Z substitutes for W.

What we need here are two elements that are pretty much interchangeable, or two elements that are unrestricted. Z and W are our two unrestricted elements, which means they can replace each other at any time without screwing things up. So, the answer is (E).

Example 5

> A chef has prepared six entrees—U, V, W, X, Y, and Z—to be served, one per night, in a certain week, starting Monday and ending Saturday. The order in which the entrees are to be served must meet the following conditions:
>
> The entrees U, V, and W, no matter what their order relative to each other, cannot be served on consecutive nights.
>
> The entrees X, Y, and Z, no matter what their order relative to each other, cannot be served on consecutive nights.
>
> U must be served earlier than in the week than Y is served.
>
> V can be served neither on Monday nor on Saturday.
>
> Z can be served neither immediately before nor immediately after V is served.

Here's the diagram:

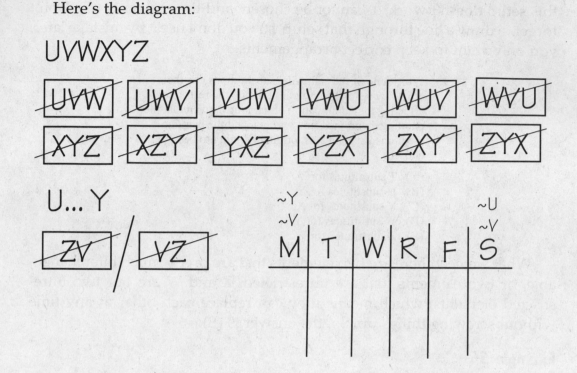

TYPE: Assignment

Hey, I know there are a lot of antiblocks up there, but it's better to write them all down than to forget one and get a question wrong. Notice the deductions on the diagram: Since U has to come before Y, Y couldn't possibly be served on Monday (if it were, where would you put U?), and U couldn't possibly be served on Saturday (if it were, where would you put Y?).

> 20. Which one of the following could be the order, from first to last, in which the entrees are served?
>
> (A) U, V, X, Y, Z, W
> (B) U, X, Z, W, Y, V
> (C) W, V, Z, U, Y, X
> **(D) X, V, W, Z, U, Y**
> (E) Z, X, V, Y, W, U

Use the clues and systematically eliminate choices. X, Y, and Z can't be in a row in any order, so (A) is out. U must be earlier in the week than Y, which eliminates (E). V can't be on Monday or Saturday, which eliminates (B). And the ZV antiblock eliminates (C). What's left? The answer, (D).

21. If Z is served on Wednesday, which one of the following must be true?

    (A) U is served on Monday

    (B) V is served on Friday.

    (C) W is served on Thursday.

    (D) X is served on Saturday.

    (E) Y is served on Saturday.

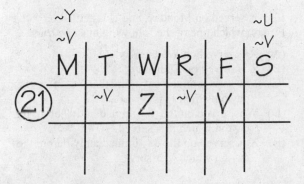

Put Z under Wednesday. Let's deal with our most restricted element, V. It can't be next to Z, which means it can't be on Tuesday or Thursday, and according to the rules, it can't be on Monday or Saturday either. So, that leaves Friday, and the answer is (B). See how cool it is to start with your most restricted element?

22. If Y is served on Wednesday, and Z is served on Thursday, then which one of the following must be true?

    (A) U is served on Tuesday.

    (B) V is served on Friday.

    (C) W is served on Friday.

    (D) W is served on Monday.

    (E) X is served on Monday.

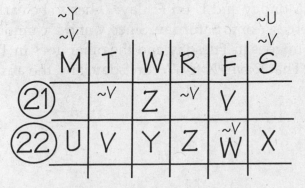

Put Y under Wednesday and Z under Thursday. We know now that V can't be on Friday, and it could never be on Monday, or Saturday. That leaves Tuesday for V (and eliminates (A) and (B) in the bargain). That forces U on Monday (eliminate (D) and (E)), since it has to come before Y. Also, since we can't have X, Y, and Z, in any order, in a row, X can't be Friday. Put X in Saturday. Who does that leave for Friday? W, so the answer is (C).

23. If W is served on Monday, and U is served on Friday, which one of the following must be true?

(A) X is served on Wednesday.
(B) Z is served on Thursday.
(C) V is served on the day immediately before the day on which U is served.
(D) W is served on the day immediately before the day on which Z is served.
(E) X is served on the day immediately before the day on which V is served.

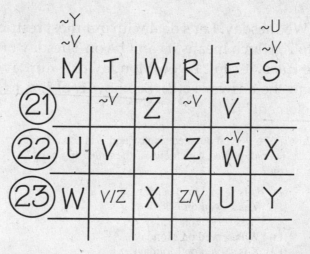

Put in W on Monday and U on Friday. U has to be earlier in the week than Y, so that forces Y onto Saturday. Since V and Z cannot be next to each other, one of them goes in Tuesday and the other goes in Thursday (order doesn't matter). That leaves X for Wednesday, and the answer is (A).

24. If X is served on the day immediately after the day on which Y is served, and immediately before the day on which W is served, then which one of the following could be true?

    (A) U is served on the day immediately before the day on which Y is served.
    (B) U is served on the day immediately before the day on which Z is served.
    (C) W is served on the day immediately before the day on which V is served.
    (D) W is served on the day immediately before the day on which Z is served.
    (E) Z is served on the day immediately before the day on which Y is served.

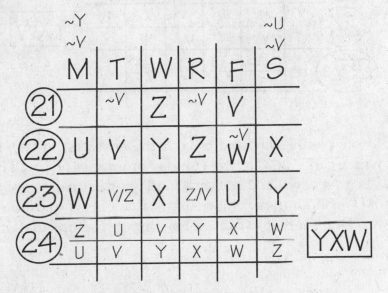

They are giving us a block for this question, and it's only true for this question. And that block is YXW. Because of the relationship U and Y have, we can expand this into U...YXW. Since Z can't be next to Y (or we'll have ZYX in a row), V must be next to Y. Now the block is UVYXW. Z is either before that block or after it. Now check out the answers. The only one possible is (D).

25. If W is served on Wednesday, any of the following could be the entree served on Thursday EXCEPT

    (A) U
    (B) V
    (C) X
    (D) Y
    (E) Z

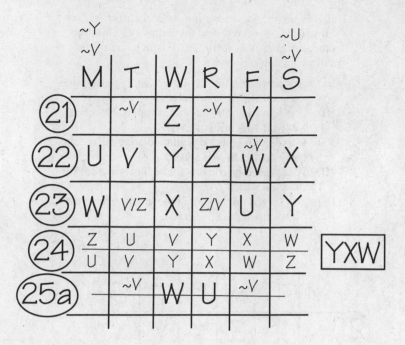

Put W in on Wednesday and try out the answers. In (A), if U is on Thursday, where can V go? Not on Tuesday or Friday (or you'll have some order of UVW in a row), and not on Monday or Saturday. So, there's no place for V if U is on Thursday. Since this is an EXCEPT question, (A) must be the answer. Don't forget to draw a line through setups that don't work.

Example 6

Eight guards—Stoddard, Thorpe, Udell, Vaughn, Westbrook, Xavier, Yates, and Zacharias—are guarding a valuable gem. They are stationed around the gem, equally spaced, in a circular formation. The following is known about their positions:

Westbrook and Xavier must be stationed next to each other.

Zacharias and Udell must be stationed next to each other.

Stoddard must be stationed directly across the circle from Yates.

Here's the diagram:

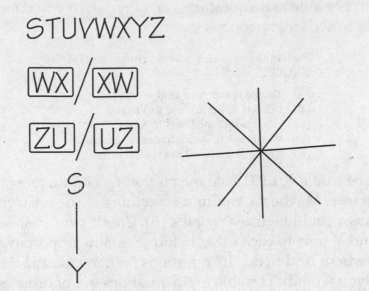

TYPE: Assignment

Notice that we don't have any information about the position of a specific guard. That means we can start anywhere on the circle. Also, hope you used this diagram instead of trying to draw a circle. You can see how this diagram makes more sense, especially with that last "across from" clue. Remember that because the diagram isn't in a line, we'll have to redraw the diagram for each "If" question. Just don't erase anything!

26. All of the following guards could be stationed immediately next to Udell EXCEPT

(A) Stoddard
(B) Thorpe
(C) Vaughn
(D) Xavier
(E) Yates

Use your past setups for this one. For other questions, we've gotten U next to Y, Z, V, and T. So, eliminate choices (B), (C), and (E). That leaves (A) and (D). So let's try (A). Is there any reason why U couldn't be stationed next to S? Nope. So the answer must be (D). Let's quickly prove it. If you put U and X next to each other, and they both bring their block pals with them, you'll have four guys in a row. This is impossible if S and Y are supposed to be across from each other. See how important it is *never* to erase your work? And to do "If" questions first, if you can? If this were the GRE CAT, you wouldn't be able to do questions out of order, so you'd just have to try the answers to see what happens.

27. Each of the following statements must be false EXCEPT

   (A) Thorpe is stationed next to Vaughn.
   (B) Udell is stationed next to Vaughn.
   (C) Udell is stationed next to Xavier.
   (D) Westbrook is stationed next to Zacharias.
   (E) Xavier is stationed next to Zacharias.

Cannot be true EXCEPT! That means you're looking for something that COULD be true. Maybe we can find something in the answers that we've already shown could be true. Yep, it's (B). Check your past setups. We've gotten U and V next to each other before. See how important it is *never* to erase your work? And to do "If" questions first, if you can? If this were the GRE CAT, you wouldn't be able to do questions out of order, so you'd just have to try the answers to see what could be true.

28. If Stoddard is stationed next to Zacharias, each of the following could be true EXCEPT

   (A) Stoddard is stationed next to Xavier.
   (B) Udell is stationed next to Thorpe.
   (C) Udell is stationed next to Yates.
   (D) Westbrook is stationed next to Yates.
   (E) Yates is stationed next to Xavier.

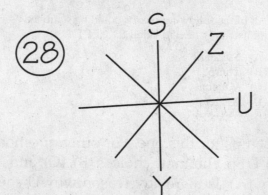

Since it doesn't matter who goes where, just put S and Z next to each other anywhere in your circle. The UZ/ZU block dictates that U goes on the other side of Z, and Y must be stationed directly across from S. That puts a space between U and Y. We may not know yet who is stationed there, but we don't have to. This is an EXCEPT question, so we're looking for something that can't be true, and we have enough information to pick choice (C). U is not next to Y.

29. If Udell and Westbrook are each stationed next to Yates, which one of the following persons could be stationed directly across the circle from Udell?

(A) Stoddard
(B) Thorpe
(C) Xavier
(D) Yates
(E) Zacharias

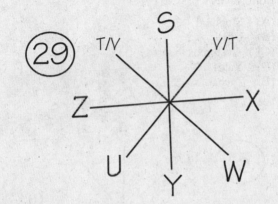

Put them in your diagram, and let's see what happens. S is across from Y, who is surrounded by W and U. X has to be on the other side of W. So, T and V are left to be in the space across from U. We don't know which one to pick, so go to the answer choices. V isn't a choice, but T is, so the answer is (B).

30. If Thorpe and Zacharias are each stationed next to Stoddard, which one of the following must be true?

(A) Thorpe is stationed across from Vaughn.
(B) Thorpe is stationed next to Westbrook.
(C) Thorpe is stationed next to Xavier.
(D) Udell is stationed next to Westbrook.
(E) Udell is stationed next to Yates.

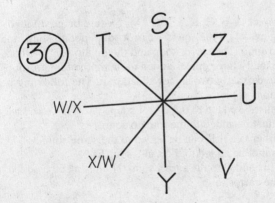

Put them in your diagram, and let's see what happens. S is across from Y, and S is surrounded by T and Z. U must be on the other side of Z (check your blocks!). Since there has to be room for the WX/XW block, V must go between U and Y. That puts V across from T, and gives us answer (A).

31. If Stoddard is stationed next to Zacharias, and if Xavier is stationed next to Yates, which one of the following people must be stationed directly across from Xavier?

(A) Stoddard
(B) Udell
(C) Westbrook
(D) Yates
(E) Zacharias

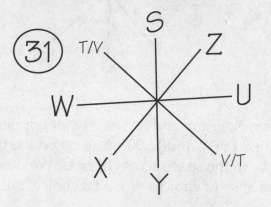

Put them in your diagram, and let's see what happens. S is across from Y, X is on one side of Y, and Z is on one side of S. Checking your blocks puts W on the other side of X, and U on the other side of Z, so T and V can fight it out for the remaining spots. Either way, the answer is (E). X and Z are across from each other.

Example 7

Eight spices—F, G, H, J, K, L, M, N—are being divided among exactly three soups—carrot soup, potato soup, and tomato soup. The carrot soup and the potato soup will each have exactly three spices added to them; the tomato soup will have exactly two spices added to it. The following conditions apply:

F must be added to the carrot soup.

G must be added to the tomato soup.

Neither G nor K can be added to the same soup as M.

J cannot be added to the same soup as N.

If H is added to the carrot soup, N must also be added to the carrot soup.

Here's the diagram:

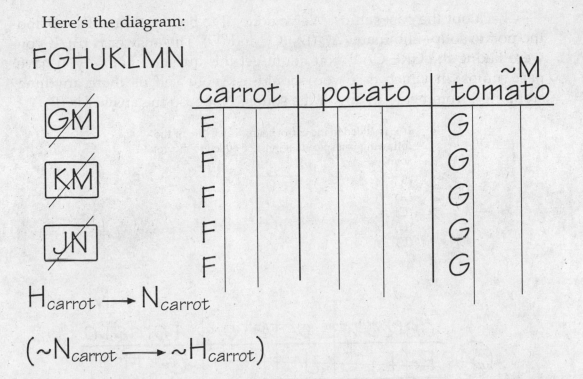

TYPE: Assignment

Note the deductions: first, that M can't be in the tomato soup, because of the GM antiblock. Next, the contrapositive of that last "if-then" clue.

32. Which one of the following is an acceptable assignment of spices to the three soups?

	carrot	potato	tomato
(A)	F, H, M	J, K, L	G, N
(B)	F, H, N	G, J, M	K, L
(C)	F, K, L	J, M, N	G, H
(D)	F, L, N	H, J, M	G, K
(E)	F, L, N	J, K, M	G, H

Check your clues in order and systematically eliminate accordingly. G must be in the tomato soup, so eliminate (B). M and K cannot be in the same soup, so eliminate (E). J and N cannot be in the same soup, so eliminate (C). If H is in the carrot soup, N must be too, so eliminate (A). That leaves us with (D), and that's our answer.

33. Which one of the following is a complete and accurate list of soups any one of which could be the soup to which J is added?

(A) carrot soup
(B) tomato soup
(C) carrot soup, tomato soup
(D) potato soup, tomato soup
(E) carrot soup, potato soup, tomato soup

Check out the past setups. We've gotten J to be in the carrot soup and the potato soup. Eliminate (A), (B), (C), and (D). The answer is (E). If you were taking the GRE CAT, you might get this question before you have past setups, in which case you should ask your self, is there anything stopping J from being in any of the soups? Nope, so the answer is (E).

34. If L is added to the carrot soup, which one of the following is a spice that must be added to the potato soup?

(A) H
(B) J
(C) K
(D) M
(E) N

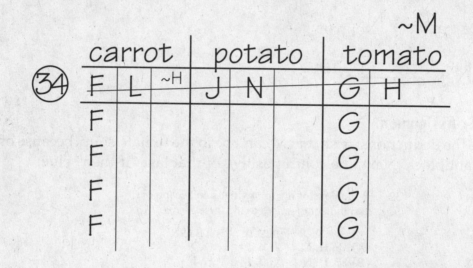

Let's deal with the tomato soup, since it's the most restricted. G is already in there, and F and L are already elsewhere. M cannot go in there (eliminate (D) and stick M somewhere else), so that leaves H, J, K, and N. Our next restricted soup is carrot, since it only has one space left. The spice that goes in that space cannot bring another spice with it (or there will be too many spices in that soup), so that spice cannot be H. Speaking of H, let's try the answers. For (A), see if you can put H somewhere other than the potato soup. Try putting H in the tomato soup. What happens? Either the JN antiblock or the MK antiblock will be violated. So, H must go in the potato soup. The answer is (A). Don't forget to draw a line through setups that don't work.

35. If L is added to the tomato soup, each of the following is a pair of spices that can be added to the carrot soup EXCEPT

(A) M and N
(B) K and N
(C) J and M
(D) J and K
(E) H and N

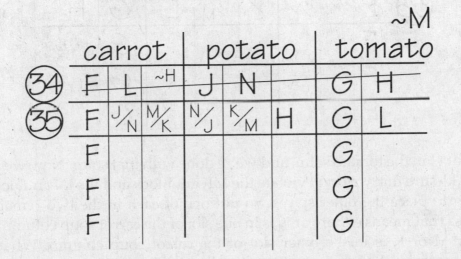

So, L goes in the tomato soup, and we're done with the tomato soup. Now we have to make sure that we don't violate the MK antiblock and the JN antiblock in trying to place the other spices. So put one of each in the two remaining soups. That means either J or N is in one slot of the carrot soup column, and either M or K is in the other slot of the carrot soup column. And H is forced into the potato soup. Check out the answers. Every one is a possible combination for the carrot soup EXCEPT H and N, so the answer is (E).

36. If H is added to the tomato soup, which one of the following is a spice that must be added to the potato soup?

(A) J
(B) K
(C) L
(D) M
(E) N

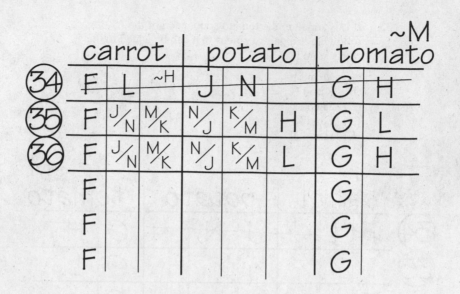

	carrot		potato		tomato	~M
③④	F ̶ L	~H	J	N	G	H
③⑤	F	J/N M/K	N/J	K/M H	G	L
③⑥	F	J/N M/K	N/J	K/M L	G	H
	F				G	
	F				G	
	F				G	

Put H in the tomato soup, and we're done with that soup. Now we have to make sure that we don't violate the MK antiblock and the JN antiblock in trying to place the other spices. So put one of each in the two remaining soups. That means either J or N is in one slot of the carrot soup column, and either M or K is in the other slot of the carrot soup column. Whatever happens there, that guarantees that L will be in the potato soup. The answer is (C).

37. Which one of the following must be true?

    (A) If H and L are added to potato soup, J is added to tomato soup.

    (B) If J and K are added to carrot soup, H is added to tomato soup.

    (C) If J and K are added to carrot soup, N is added to tomato soup.

    (D) If J and L are added to carrot soup, K is added to tomato soup.

    (E) If M and N are added to potato soup, L is added to potato soup.

Well, just try them. In (A), if you put H and L in the potato soup, can you put J somewhere else? Sure, you can put it in the carrot soup. Eliminate (A). In (B), if you put J and K in the carrot soup, can you put H somewhere other than the tomato soup? Sure, you can put it in the potato soup. Eliminate (B). In (C), if you put J and K in the carrot soup, can you put N somewhere other than the tomato soup? Sure, you can put it in the potato soup. Eliminate (C). In (D), if you put J and L in the carrot soup, can you put K somewhere other than the tomato soup? Actually, no. Bingo. The answer is (D).

Example 8

A certain race involves nine athletes: King, Leighton, Maynard, Nguyen, Oakley, Phelan, Quigley, Reilly, and Shea.

> Oakley and Reilly run at the same time as each other, and no one else runs at that time.
>
> Leighton and Phelan run at the same time as each other, and no one else runs at that time.
>
> No other athlete runs at the same time as another athlete.
>
> Nguyen runs before King.
>
> Quigley runs before Maynard.
>
> Maynard runs after Reilly but before Nguyen.
>
> Phelan runs after both Shea and King.
>
> King runs before Shea.

Here's the diagram:

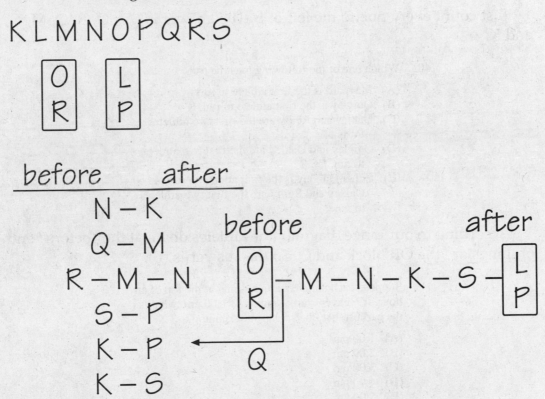

TYPE: Non-Assignment, Range

First, symbolize all the clues separately, keeping track of "before" and "after." Then, combine all the clues to make the longest chain possible. The good thing about games like this one is that once you draw your diagram, you never really have to touch it again.

38. Who are the last two athletes to run?

   (A) Nguyen and Shea
   (B) King and Phelan
   (C) King and Leighton
   (D) Phelan and Leighton
   (E) Shea and King

According to our range diagram, P and L both end up at the "after" end of things. So, the answer is (D).

39. Exactly how many athletes run before Shea?

   (A) 6
   (B) 5
   (C) 4
   (D) 3
   (E) 2

Just count every one to the left of S. The answer is (A); O, R, Q, M, N, and K.

40. Which one of the following must be true?

   (A) Maynard is the first athlete to run.
   (B) Quigley is the first athlete to run.
   (C) Oakley and Reilly are the first two athletes
        to run.
   (D) Quigley and Oakley are the first two athletes
        to run.
   (E) Either Quigley is the first athlete to run or
        Oakley and Reilly are the first two athletes
        to run.

According to our range diagram, the athletes down at the "before" end of things are the OR block and Q. So the answer is (E).

41. Suppose each athlete starts running at the top of an
    hour. If Nguyen starts running at 1:00 pm, what is
    the earliest that Phelan can start running?

   (A) 1:00 pm
   (B) 2:00 pm
   (C) 3:00 pm
   (D) 4:00 pm
   (E) 5:00 pm

Ooh, the dreaded "Suppose" question. K, S, and the PL block still have to come after N, so the earliest P (and L) could have run is 4 pm. That's (D).

Example 9

Six offices in a publishing company are on the same floor, which is laid out as follows:

    101 102
    103 104
    105 106

The eight employees who could share these offices are:
    four editors, two proofreaders, and two graphic artists.
    The locations of these employees are subject to the
    following conditions:
 ✳No employee is in more than one of the offices.
    None of the offices contains more than one proofreader,
        and none contains more than one graphic artist.
    None of the offices contains both a proofreader and a
        graphic artist.
    Each proofreader is located in an office that contains at
        least one editor.
    The graphic artists are located in two offices that are not
        directly across from, to the left of, or to the right of
        each other.
    Office 103 contains a graphic artist, and office 106
        contains a proofreader.

Here's the diagram:

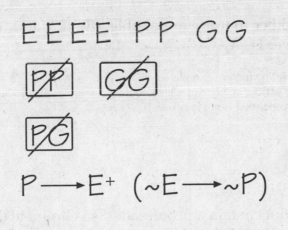

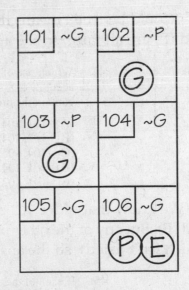

TYPE: Assignment

You MUST put asterisks next to the clues you didn't symbolize. The deduction here is that there's a G in office 102. Why? Because there's a G in 103, and since the G offices can't be directly across, to the right of or to the left of each other, there can't be a G in 101, 104, or 105. There can't be a G in 106 either, because there's a P in there (remember the GP antiblock). So, a G is in 102 by default, and we're done with the Gs. Also, since every P has to be accompanied by at least one E, there's an E in 106. Don't forget your contrapositives and other restrictions (no Ps in 102 and 103, because of the GP antiblock). And remember, you'll have to redraw this diagram for each "If" question.

42. Which one of the following could be true?

(A) Office 105 contains a graphic artist.
(B) Office 106 contains a graphic artist.
(C) Office 102 contains a proofreader.
(D) Office 103 contains a proofreader.
(E) Office 103 contains an editor.

"Could be true" means the other four are impossible. (A), (B), (C), and (D) are all false, so the answer is (E).

43. Which one of the following could be true?

(A) Office 101 contains exactly one editor.
(B) Office 101 contains exactly one graphic artist.
(C) Office 102 contains exactly one proofreader.
(D) Office 105 contains exactly one graphic artist.
(E) Office 106 contains exactly one graphic artist.

"Could be true" means the other four are impossible. (B), (C), and (D) and (E) are all false, so the answer is (A).

44. Which one of the following is a complete and accurate list of the offices any one of which could contain the proofreader that is not in office 106?

(A) 101, 104
(B) 102, 104
(C) 104, 105
(D) 101, 104, 105
(E) 101, 102, 104, 105

We know that office 102 cannot contain a proofreader, so eliminate (B) and (E). But any of the other offices could contain a proofreader (except 103, which isn't listed), so the answer is (D).

45. If each of the six offices contains at least one of the eight employees, then which one of the following must be true?

(A) There is a proofreader in office 101.
(B) There is an editor in office 102.
(C) There is an editor in office 103.
(D) There is an editor in office 104.
(E) There is a proofreader in office 104.

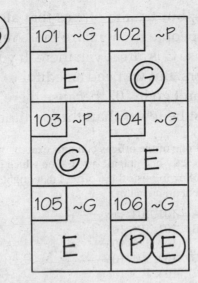

Let's fill up the spaces with the elements we have the most of—the editors. Put one in each empty office: 101, 104, and 105. That extra proof-reader can go in any of those offices too, but whatever happens, there's an editor in 104, which is (D).

46. In which one of the following offices must there be fewer than three editors?

(A) 101
(B) 102
(C) 104
(D) 105
(E) 106

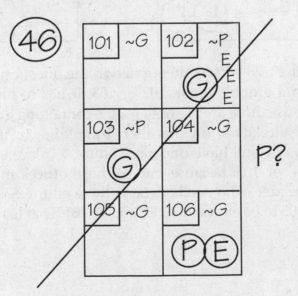

Try the answers, but try the offices that already have people in them. Why? Offices with people in them are more restricted than empty offices. Start with (B), because G is already in there. If you put three editors in there, that's it for the editors. But we need an editor to go with the as yet unplaced proofreader, who can't go in 102, because there's already a graphic artist in there. So, there must be fewer than three editors in 102. The answer is (B).

47. If one of the offices contains exactly two editors and exactly one graphic artist, then which one of the following lists three offices that might, among them, contain no editor?

(A) 101, 103, 105
(B) 101, 104, 105
(C) 102, 103, 105
(D) 102, 104, 106
(E) 104, 105, 106

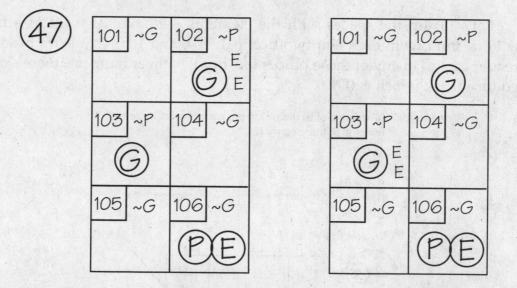

You can put the two editors mentioned in the question in either of the rooms containing a graphic artist: 102 or 103. It has to happen in one of those rooms, because those are the only rooms containing graphic artists, so eliminate (C). We already know that there's an editor in 106, so eliminate (D) and (E). Now, we still have one more editor to place, and it has to go either in 101, 104, or 105, because one of those offices must contain the remaining proofreader, who needs to be with an editor. So, it's impossible for 101, 104 and 105 to be editor-free. Eliminate (B). That leaves us with (A).

Example 10

In a shelving unit, there are exactly eight shelves, arranged vertically and numbered consecutively 1 (bottom), through 8 (top). Exactly six vases—B, C, D, F, G, and H—are to be placed on the shelves according to the following conditions:

No more than one vase can be placed on any shelf.
B must be placed on a lower-numbered shelf than G.
C and H, not necessarily in that order, must be placed on shelves immediately above or below each other.
Any shelf immediately above or below the shelf on which F is placed must remain empty.

Here's the diagram:

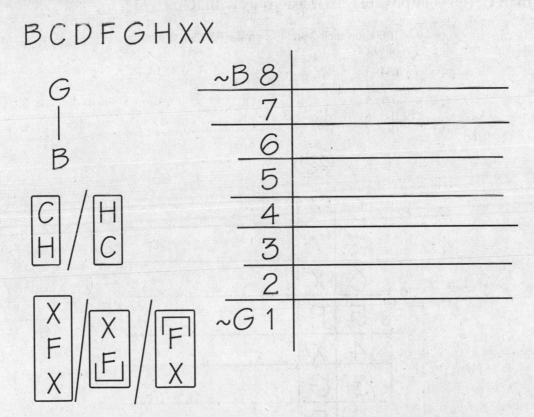

TYPE: Assignment

Don't panic, it's just vertical, but it's still a grid. And our blocks are vertical too. Notice the "empties" are symbolized with two Xs. Because B has to be lower than G, we can deduce that G can't be on the bottom shelf and B can't be on the top shelf. Now, it gets a little tricky with F. Either F is surrounded by the two empties, OR F is on the bottom shelf and there's an empty on 2, OR F is on the top shelf and there's an empty on 7.

48. If shelves 1 through 4 all hold vases, which one of the following could be the four vases, in order from shelf 1 to shelf 4, on those four shelves?

    (A) C, B, G, D
    (B) C, H, B, F
    (C) D, B, G, H
    (D) D, G, H, C
    (E) F, B, G, C

Since F is connected to those empty shelves, it can't be in the correct answer to this question. So, eliminate (B) and (E). Let's continue checking our clues. Well, we have the CH/HC block (yes, blocks can be vertical), which would eliminate (A). And, since B must be placed on a lower shelf than G, (D) is impossible. That leaves us with (C).

49. If D is on shelf 2 and F is on shelf 5, then G must be on shelf

    (A) 3
    (B) 4
    (C) 5
    (D) 6
    (E) 7

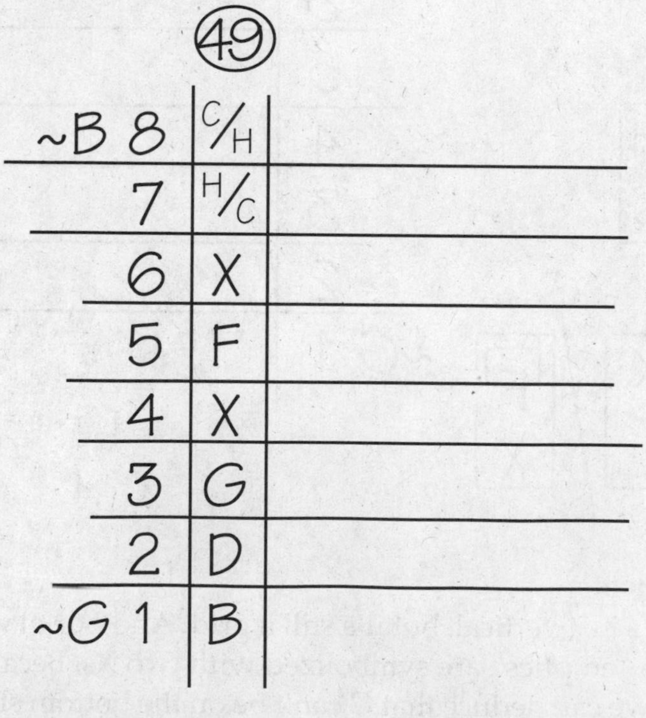

㊾

~B	8	C/H
	7	H/C
	6	X
	5	F
	4	X
	3	G
	2	D
~G	1	B

Put D on 2 on F on 5, and don't forget to put empty symbols on 4 and 6. Now we move on to the block. The only place there's room for the CH/HC block is on 7 and 8 (order doesn't matter). Since B has to be on a lower shelf than G, that puts B on 1 and G on 3. So, our answer is (A).

50. If shelves 3 and 7 are empty and G is on shelf 5, which one of the following must be true?

   (A) B is on shelf 1.
   (B) C is on shelf 1.
   (C) D is on shelf 6.
   (D) D is on shelf 8.
   (E) F is on shelf 2.

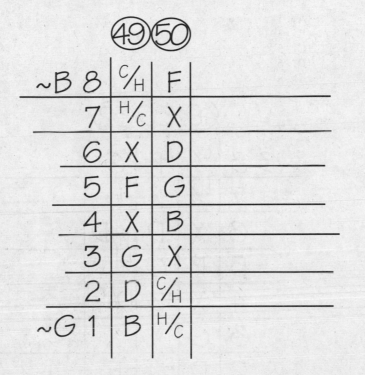

At first you might have thought this was a typo; doesn't F have to be surrounded by empties? Well, what if F is on 8 and there's an empty on 7? Doesn't that conform with the rules of the game? Yep. So, put F on 8, put in empties at 3 and 7, and G on 5. Now we move on to the block. The only place there's room for the CH/HC block is on 1 and 2 (order doesn't matter). B has to be lower than G, so B must go on 4. That leaves 6 for D. The answer is (C).

51. If B is on the only shelf between the two empty shelves, which one of the following must be true?

   (A) B is on shelf 6.
   (B) F is on shelf 1.
   (C) G is on a shelf immediately above or below an
       empty shelf.
   (D) Shelf 3 is empty.
   (E) Shelf 5 is empty.

This means that it has to go FXBX on 1, 2, 3, and 4, respectively. That's the only way to deal with both F's and B's restrictions. It can't go XBXF on 5, 6, 7, and 8, respectively, because B has to be below G, and where would you put G? So, the answer is (B).

52. If F is on shelf 2 and B is on shelf 7, then D could be on shelf

(A) 1
(B) 3
(C) 5
(D) 6
(E) 8

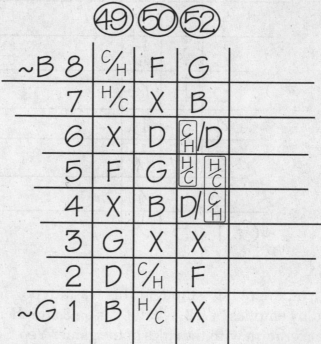

F on 2 means empties on 1 and 3. B on 7 means G has to be on 8. Now let's deal with the CH/HC block. It can either go on 4 and 5 or 5 and 6. Either way, either C or H is on 5. So, we've definitely got something in every space except 4 and 6. So D can be on either 4 or 6. Since 4 is not a choice, go for 6, and choice (D).

53. If F is on shelf 6, then any of the following could be true EXCEPT:

(A) B is on shelf 3.
(B) C is on shelf 8.
(C) D is on shelf 8.
(D) G is on shelf 2.
(E) H is on shelf 4.

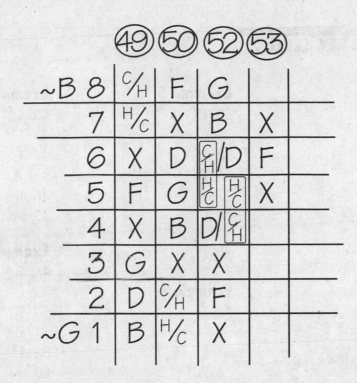

F on 6 means empties on 5 and 7. We don't really know much else, so check out the answers and find one that isn't possible. It's (B), because of the CH/HC block. If C were on 8, where would you put H? Shelf 7 isn't an option, because there's an empty there. (B) is our answer.

54. If C and H are on the only two shelves between the two empty shelves, then D could be on any of the following shelves EXCEPT shelf

(A) 1
(B) 3
(C) 4
(D) 7
(E) 8

This implies that F is on an end, so let's try it on 1. So, there's an empty on 2, then the CH/HC block on 3 and 4, and then another empty. That gives D the option of 6, 7, or 8. So, you can eliminate choices (D) and (E). Now try it with F on 8. There's an empty on 7, then the CH/HC block on 6 and 5, and the other empty on 4. That gives D the option of 1, 2, or 3. Now eliminate choices (A) and (B). That leaves you with the answer, (C).

ANSWER KEY, LEVEL 2

Example 1
1. B
2. A
3. C
4. B
5. B
6. C

Example 2
7. D
8. B
9. A
10. A
11. E
12. A

Example 3
13. B
14. A
15. B
16. D

Example 4
17. E
18. D
19. B
20. D
21. B
22. A

Example 5
23. D
24. C
25. E
26. B
27. A
28. C
29. A
30. C

Example 6
31. D
32. E
33. C
34. A
35. B
36. E

Example 7
37. B
38. C
39. C
40. C
41. E

Example 8
42. C
43. E
44. E
45. A
46. B
47. A

Example 9
48. B
49. C
50. E
51. B
52. D
53. A

Example 10
54. C
55. D
56. E
57. E
58. C
59. E

EXPLANATIONS, LEVEL 2

Example 1

A night club is scheduling its early and late shows for Thursday, Friday, Saturday, and Sunday of a certain week. Each show will feature exactly one of the following five bands: The Night Owls, The Parrots, The Quiet Men, The Right Stuff, and The Wobbles.

* No band will be featured during a late show more than once during the week.

* No band will be featured during an early show more than once during the week.

On Thursday, only The Quiet Men, The Right Stuff, or The Wobbles will be featured.

On Friday, only The Night Owls or The Wobbles will be featured.

On Saturday, only The Parrots, The Quiet Men, The Right Stuff, or The Wobbles will be featured.

On Sunday, only The Parrots, The Quiet Men, or The Wobbles will be featured.

The early show and the late show cannot feature the same band on the same night.

The Wobbles are featured on the late show on Sunday.

Here's the diagram:

NPQRW

	$\sim$P $\sim$N		$\sim$N	$\sim$N $\sim$R
	T Q/R	F	Sa P/Q/R	Su P/Q
early	Q/R	W		P/Q
late	R/Q	N		W
early				
late				
early				
late				

TYPE: Assignment

Lots of deductions here. First, make sure you put the restrictions above the diagram. Next, don't forget to put asterisks next to clues that can't be symbolized. Now, we know that W goes in the late Sunday slot. We now know that no other late slot can feature W. Since Friday's only options are N and W, the N must go on late, and the W must go on early. These deductions mean that the early and late Thursday shows can only feature either Q or R, and the early Sunday show can only feature either P or Q. Since this diagram has two levels, we can't fill in all the way down the definitely placed elements. Put circles around them instead, so you remember to repeat them in subsequent setups.

1. Which one of the following statements must be true?

   (A) The Right Stuff is featured during the early show on Thursday.
   (B) The Wobbles are featured during the early show on Friday.
   (C) The Quiet Men are featured during the early show on Saturday.
   (D) The Quiet Men are featured during the late show on Thursday.
   (E) The Parrots are featured during the late show on Saturday.

This was a deduction, but let's go over it again. Sunday's late show is The Wobbles. Go to the most restricted day, which is Friday. Friday can either feature The Night Owls or The Wobbles, and The Wobbles can't be on the late show, because The Wobbles are already doing Sunday's late show. So, The Night Owls do Friday's late show, and The Wobbles do Friday's early show. That's (B).

2. It CANNOT be true that, during the week, both the early show and the late show feature which one of the following bands?

   (A) The Night Owls
   (B) The Parrots
   (C) The Quiet Men
   (D) The Right Stuff
   (E) The Wobbles

Which of our bands is most restricted? In other words, which one can't be in the most places? It's The Night Owls. In fact, The Night Owls can only be featured during Friday's late show. That's (A). Whenever you get stuck, always start with your most restricted elements or places.

3. If The Right Stuff is featured during the early show
    on Thursday, then which one of the following
    statements must be true?

    (A) The Parrots are featured during the early show
         on Saturday.
    (B) The Quiet Men are featured during the early
         show on Sunday.
    (C) The Quiet Men are featured during the late
         show on Thursday.
    (D) The Parrots are featured during the late show on
         Saturday.
    (E) The Right Stuff is featured during the late show
         on Saturday.

	~P ~N		~N	~N ~R
	T	**F**	**Sa**	**Su**
	Q/R	N	P/Q/R	P/Q
early	Q/R	(W)		P/Q
late	R/Q	(N)		(W)
early	R	(W)	P/Q	P/Q
late	Q	(N)		(W)
early				
late				
early				
late				

③

If The Right Stuff does the early show on Thursday, only Q can do the
late show. We deduced that only Q and R can do the Thursday shows, and
if R does the early one, Q has to do the late one. The answer is (C).

4. Which one of the following statements could be true?

    (A) Neither The Quiet Men nor The Right Stuff is
         featured during the early show on Thursday.
    (B) Neither The Quiet Men nor The Right Stuff is
         featured during the early show on Saturday.
    (C) Neither The Parrots nor The Quiet Men are
         featured during the early show on Sunday.
    (D) Neither The Quiet Men nor The Right Stuff is
         featured during the late show on Thursday.
    (E) Neither The Parrots, nor The Quiet Men, nor
         The Right Stuff is featured during the late
         show on Saturday.

"Could be true" means the other four are impossible. So, let's check out
the answers. Is it possible for neither The Quiet Men nor The Right Stuff to
do Thursday's early show? No, we've already deduced that either The
Quiet Men or The Right Stuff MUST do the early show on Thursday. (A)
cannot be true, so eliminate it. On to (B). Is it possible for neither The Quiet
Men nor The Right Stuff to do the early show on Saturday? Is there anyone
else who could do it? Sure, how about The Parrots? No problem. So (B) is
the answer, because it could be true.

5. If The Right Stuff is never featured during a late
    show, then which one of the following statements
    must be false?

    (A) The Right Stuff is featured during the early
         show on Thursday.
    (B) The Right Stuff is featured during the early
         show on Saturday.
    (C) The Parrots are featured during the early show
         on Sunday.
    (D) The Quiet Men are featured during the late
         show on Thursday.
    (E) The Parrots are featured during the late show on
         Saturday.

	~P ~N **T** Q/R	**F**	~N **Sa** P/Q/R	~N ~R **Su** P/Q
early	Q/R	Ⓦ		P/Q
late	R/Q	Ⓝ		Ⓦ
③ early	R	Ⓦ	P/Q	P/Q
③ late	Q	Ⓝ		Ⓦ
⑤ early	R	Ⓦ	Q	P
⑤ late	~R Q	Ⓝ	~R P	Ⓦ
early				
late				

We need to fill in the late show without using The Right Stuff. We have no choice but to have The Quiet Men do Thursday's late show (eliminate (D) because it must be true). That forces The Parrots to do Saturday's late show (eliminate (E) because it must be true). The Right Stuff will have to do Thursday's early show (eliminate (A) because it must be true). The Quiet Men will have to do Saturday's early show. This forces The Parrots to do Sunday's early show (eliminate (C) because it must be true). That means (B) must be false, so that's the answer.

6. Which one of the following statements could be true?

    (A)   The Quiet Men are featured during the early show on Thursday and The Right Stuff is featured during the late show on Saturday.

    (B)   The Right Stuff is featured during the early show on Saturday and The Quiet Men are featured during the early show on Sunday.

    (C)   The Quiet Men are featured during the early show on Saturday and The Quiet Men are featured during the late show on Thursday.

    (D)   The Right Stuff is featured during the early show on Saturday and The Quiet Men are featured during the late show on Thursday.

    (E)   The Quiet Men are featured during the early show on Sunday and The Quiet Men are featured during the late show on Saturday.

Let's check out the answers, because "could be true" means the other four are impossible. In (A), having The Quiet Men do Thursday's early show forces The Right Stuff to do Thursday's late show, so The Right Stuff can't do any other late show. Eliminate (A). In (B), having The Right Stuff do Saturday's early show forces The Right Stuff to do Thursday's late show, and The Quiet Men to do Thursday's early show. That means The Quiet Men can't do any other early shows, so eliminate (B). In (C), having The Quiet Men do Saturday's early show forces The Right Stuff to do Thursday's early show, which forces The Quiet Men to do Thursday's late show. Looks good. (C)'s the answer.

Example 2

On the third floor of a professional building, there are four offices on one side of the hall, labeled A, C, E, and G, and four offices on the opposite side of the hall, labeled consecutively B, D, F, and H. Offices B, D, F, and H will face offices A, C, E, and G, respectively. Each office will belong to exactly one of three types of professionals—psychologists, lawyers, or orthodontists—according to the following conditions:

Adjacent offices must belong to different types of professionals.
No lawyer's office faces another lawyer's office.
Every psychologist's office has at least one orthodontist's office adjacent to it.
Office C is a psychologist's office.
Office F is a lawyer's office.

Here's the diagram:

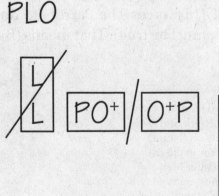

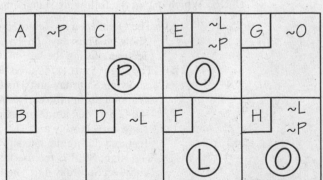

TYPE: Assignment

Okay, we know that P goes in C and L goes in F. We now know that A can't have P in it. Since L's can't be facing each other, we know that E can't have L in it. E also can't have P in it, because adjacent offices can't contain the same type of professional. So, E can't have L and it can't have P, so it must have O. That means G can't have O. Now, H can't have L, because F has L (adjacent offices can't contain the same type of professional). H also cannot have P, because every P has to have an O next to it, and since H is on the end, and an L is next to it, there's no way H can contain P. That means H contains O. Don't forget that you'll have to redraw this diagram for every "If" question, copying over all the original information. That's why we're circling stuff.

7. Any of the following could be an orthodontist's office EXCEPT office

    (A) A
    (B) B
    (C) D
    (D) G
    (E) H

First, we know that E and H have to be orthodontists' offices, so eliminate (E). We also know that G cannot be, because adjacent offices must belong to different types of professionals. Since this is an EXCEPT question, the answer is (D). Anyway, wasn't this a deduction? Yes, but in case you didn't make it, now you have it.

8. If there is one psychologist's office directly opposite another psychologist's office, which one of the following could be true?

    (A) Office H is a psychologist's office.
    (B) Office G is a lawyer's office.
    (C) Office D is an orthodontist's office.
    (D) Office B is a lawyer's office.
    (E) Office A is a psychologist's office.

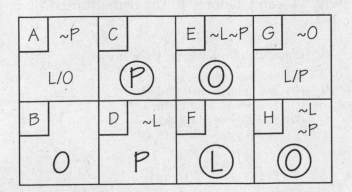

First, to satisfy the question, put a P in office D, which forces an orthodontist in B. Now you can eliminate (C) and (D). Now, check out the rest of the answers: "could be true" means the other four are impossible. We already know that H belongs to an orthodontist, so eliminate (A). We already know that A can't belong to a psychologist, because C does, so eliminate (E). We're left with (B), so that has to be it. Besides, do we know for sure who's in G? Nope, it could be a lawyer, so (B) is definitely the answer.

9. If office D is an orthodontist's office, then it could be true that office

    (A) A is an orthodontist's office
    (B) B is an orthodontist's office
    (C) E is a psychologist's office
    (D) G is an orthodontist's office
    (E) H is a psychologist's office

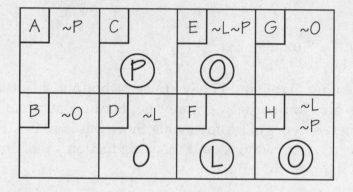

Put an O in D. That means that for this question, B can't belong to an orthodontist. Eliminate (B). Now, check out the rest of the answers: "could be true" means the other four are impossible. We already know that H belongs to an orthodontist, so eliminate (E). We already know that E belongs to an orthodontist, so eliminate (C). We already know that G cannot belong to an orthodontist, so eliminate (D). That leaves us with (A). Any reason why A can't belong to an orthodontist? Nope. That's the answer.

10. On the third floor, there could be exactly

    (A) one psychologist's office
    (B) one orthodontist's office
    (C) two orthodontist's offices
    (D) four psychologist's offices
    (E) five psychologist's offices

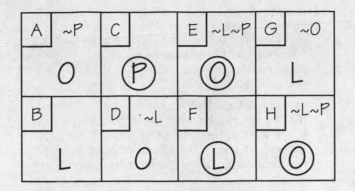

Try them. In (A), is there a way to fill out the whole diagram with only one P? Sure, put Os in A and D (remember, they're already in E and H). Put Ls in B and G (there's already one in F). That's it! The answer is (A).

11. If no office occupied by a certain professional faces an office occupied by a professional of the same type, then it must be true that office

(A) A is a lawyer's office
(B) A is an orthodontist's office
(C) B is a psychologist's office
(D) B is a lawyer's office
(E) D is an orthodontist's office

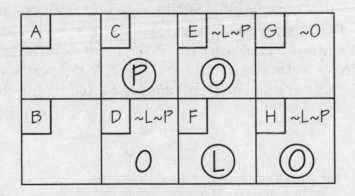

This question is telling us that D can't belong to a psychologist. It also can't belong to a lawyer, which we knew from the beginning. That means it must belong to an orthodontist. That's (E).

12. If the condition requiring office F to be a lawyer's office is no longer true but all other original conditions remain the same, then any of the following could be an accurate list of the professionals occupying offices B, D, F, and H, respectively, EXCEPT:

(A) psychologist, lawyer, psychologist, orthodontist
(B) lawyer, psychologist, orthodontist, lawyer
(C) lawyer, orthodontist, psychologist, lawyer
(D) orthodontist, psychologist, orthodontist, lawyer
(E) orthodontist, lawyer, psychologist, orthodontist

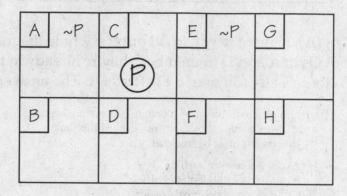

Hey, this is really a "Suppose" question, isn't it? They are taking away a condition. That means that any deductions we made based on that condition are also gone. So this is all we can do with our diagram. But everything else is still intact. For example, it's still true that every psychologist's office has at least one orthodontist's office adjacent to it. Now, how do we feel about (A)? It has a psychologist next to a lawyer, not an orthodontist. That's no good, and this is an EXCEPT question, so (A) is the answer.

Example 3

A zoo uses a tram to connect the seven different animal areas. There are two-way roads connecting each of the following pairs of points: 1 with 2, 1 with 3, 1 with 5, 2 with 6, 3 with 7, 5 with 6, and 6 with 7. There are also one-way roads going from 2 to 4, from 3 to 2, and from 4 to 3. There are no other roads in the network, and the roads in the network do not intersect.

When traveling from one area to another, the tram must take the route that for the whole trip passes through the fewest of the points 1 through 7, counting a point twice if the tram passes through it twice.

The pandas are at point 3. The tigers are at point 1, the gorillas at point 5, and the birds are at point 4. The zebras are at point 2, the lions are at point 6, and the reptiles are at point 7.

Here's the diagram:

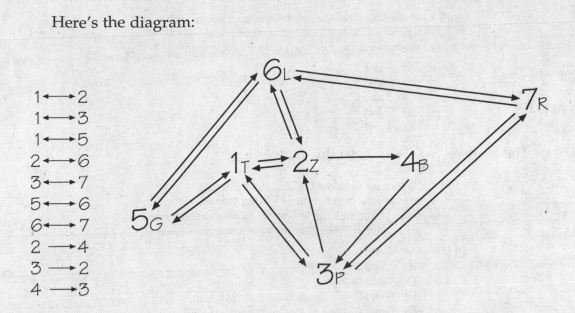

1 ←→ 2
1 ←→ 3
1 ←→ 5
2 ←→ 6
3 ←→ 7
5 ←→ 6
6 ←→ 7
2 ——→ 4
3 ——→ 2
4 ——→ 3

TYPE: Non-Assignment, Path/Map

Symbolize each connection separately, then put them together any way you want, as long as the connections follow the conditions. Your diagram might have looked slightly different from this one, but that's okay. Make the diagram any way you want, just as long as the *right* connections are made. Also, don't mistake these arrows for "if-then" arrows. These are just regular directional arrows. Notice that some arrows only point in one direction, while others point in both directions. Remember, the nice thing about a game like this is that once you draw the diagram, you never have to touch it again.

13. If the tram starts at the tigers and goes to the reptiles, the first intermediate point on the route must be

   (A) 2
   (B) 3
   (C) 5
   (D) 6
   (E) 7

The shortest route from the tigers to the reptiles would be 1-3-7, so we're passing through 3, which is (B).

14. If, starting from the pandas, the tram goes to the tigers and the birds, (in either order), and ends up at the reptiles, the first two points on the route must be

(A) 1 and 2
(B) 1 and 3
(C) 2 and 1
(D) 2 and 4
(E) 4 and 2

The route is 3-1-2-4-3-7, so the answer is (A).

15. If, starting from the gorillas, the tram goes to the tigers or the birds next (whichever stop requires the route go through the fewest of the points) and then goes to the reptiles, the first two on the route must be

(A) 1 and 2
(B) 1 and 3
(C) 4 and 2
(D) 6 and 2
(E) 6 and 4

The route is 5-1-3-7, so the answer is (B).

16. If the tram makes a trip starting at the reptiles, going to the birds, and then ending at the lions, the first two points on the route could be

(A) 3 and 1
(B) 3 and 4
(C) 4 and 2
(D) 6 and 2
(E) 6 and 5

The route can either be 7-3-2-4-3-2-6 or 7-6-2-4-3-2-6. The only choice represented by either of these routes is (D), 6 and 2.

Example 4

An automobile company is showing five vehicles—a family car, a pickup truck, a recreational vehicle, a sports car, and a van—on one night for a promotional event. Each vehicle must be a different color—black, green, orange, tan, and white. The following restrictions apply:

The white vehicle is shown fourth.
The black vehicle and the green vehicle are, in either order, shown immediately before and after the sports car.
There are exactly two vehicles between the recreational vehicle and the green vehicle.
The van is shown after the pickup truck.

Here's the diagram:

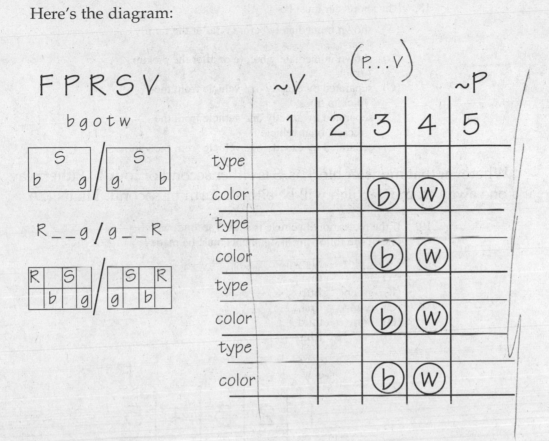

TYPE: Assignment

There are huge blocks in this game. Since both of those big blocks contain green, we combined them and got the monster block on the bottom. Whichever direction that block goes in, the third vehicle will have to be black (try it and see!). Don't forget to circle any element that's been permanently placed.

17. Which one of the following is a possible order of vehicle colors?

	First	Second	Third	Fourth	Fifth
(A)	black	green	orange	white	tan
(B)	green	orange	tan	white	black
(C)	green	white	black	tan	orange
(D)	orange	tan	green	white	black
(E)	tan	orange	black	white	green

We know that the white car is shown fourth, so eliminate (C). We deduced that the third car must be black, so eliminate (A), (B), and (D). That's it! The answer is (E).

18. The sports car must be

   (A) shown immediately before or after the family car
   (B) shown immediately before or after the pickup truck
   (C) separated by exactly one vehicle from the pickup truck
   (D) separated by exactly one vehicle from the recreational vehicle
   (E) separated by exactly one vehicle from the van

Wherever that monster block is, S is either second or fourth. Either way, it's one away from R, which will be either fourth or second. That's (D).

19. If the recreational vehicle is shown second, which one of the following assignments must be made?

	Color	Shown
(A)	black	first
(B)	green	fifth
(C)	orange	first
(D)	orange	third
(E)	tan	fifth

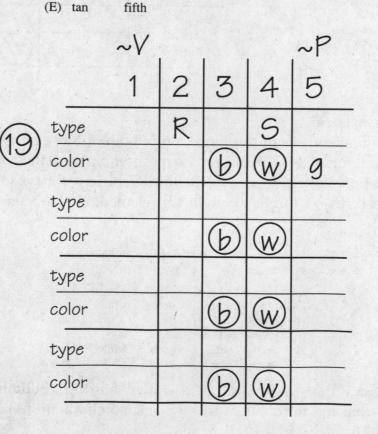

They've placed that monster block for us, and green is in fifth. The answer is (B).

20. Which one of the following is a complete and
     accurate list of vehicles each of which could be
     black?

   (A) family car, pickup truck
   (B) sports car, van
   (C) family car, pickup truck, recreational vehicle
   (D) family car, pickup truck, van
   (E) pickup truck, sports car, van

We deduced that black is third, and that monster block dictates that the black car is between the recreational vehicle and the sports car, so neither of those can be black. Eliminate any choice that includes either the recreational vehicle or the sports car. (B), (C), and (E) are out. Now, is there any reason any of the remaining vehicles can't be black? Nope. So, the answer is (D).

21. If the pickup truck is tan, then it must be true that

   (A) the green vehicle is shown first.
   (B) the orange vehicle is shown second.
   (C) the family car is white.
   (D) the recreational vehicle is black.
   (E) the sports car is orange.

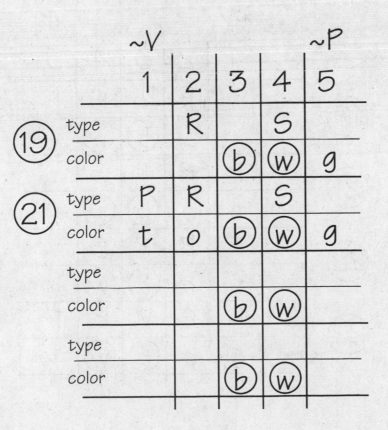

Remember that the van is shown later than the pickup truck, so the pickup truck can't be fifth. This means the tan pickup truck will have to be first, followed by the monster block, with the recreational vehicle in the second position. The only color we haven't filled in is orange, and the only space for it is second, so the answer is (B).

22. If the family car is tan, which one of the following could represent the order in which the vehicles are shown?

	First	Second	Third	Fourth	Fifth
(A)	family car	recreational vehicle	pickup truck	sports car	van
(B)	family car	pickup truck	recreational vehicle	van	sports car
(C)	family car	van	sports car	pickup truck	recreational vehicle
(D)	pickup truck	recreational vehicle	family car	sports car	van
(E)	pickup truck	van	recreational vehicle	sports car	family car

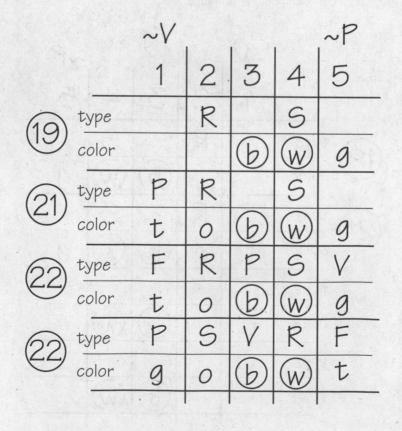

We can put the tan family car either first or last. If it's first, and the monster block follows, the order of the vehicles looks like (A). (If we put it last, the set is PSVRF, which is not a choice). So, the answer is (A).

Example 5

The student jury at the university will consist of exactly five members, one of whom will be its foreman. The members will be appointed from among a group of five graduate students—B, C, D, E, and F—and a group of four undergraduate students—M, N, O, and P. The following conditions must be met:

* The student jury must include at least two appointees from each group.
* The foreman must be a member belonging to the group from which exactly two members are appointed.
   If B is appointed, N must be appointed.
   If C is appointed, E must be appointed.
   If either D or F is appointed, the other must also appointed.
   F and M cannot both be appointed.

Here's the diagram:

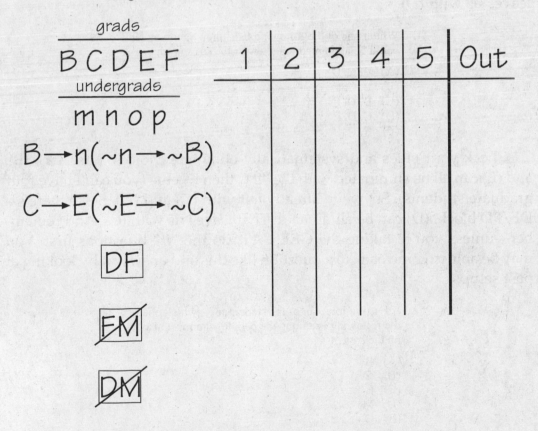

TYPE: Assignment

Since not everyone gets on this jury, we need an "out" column. We've got our contrapositive deductions in parentheses next to the corresponding clues. Notice that the clue about D and F is really a block. Are you wondering where that DM antiblock came from? Well, if D and F must be in, and F and M can't both be in, what can you deduce? That D and M can't both be in. It is CRUCIAL to put asterisks next to the clues you didn't symbolize.

23. Which one of the following is an acceptable selection of members for the student jury?

    (A) B, C, N, O, P
    (B) B, D, E, M, N
    (C) B, M, N, O, P
    (D) D, E, F, N, P
    (E) D, F, M, N, P

Check your clues and systematically eliminate choices. First, there have to be two members from each group, and that eliminates choice (C). If you have C, you have to have E, so that gets rid of (A). D and F are in a block, which gets rid of (B). And, F and M are in an antiblock, so (E) is gone. That leaves us with (D).

24. Which one of the following lists three members who could be appointed together for the student jury?

    (A) B, C, D
    (B) B, C, F
    (C) B, D, F
    (D) C, D, E
    (E) C, D, F

Check your clues and systematically eliminate choices. First, (A), (B), and (E) can all be eliminated with the "if C then E" clue (you can't have four graduate students). So, we're already left with (C) and (D). Since there's a DF/FD block, (D) can be eliminated. That leaves us with (C). And remember—unless you're taking the GRE CAT, do the "if" questions first. You may be able to come back to a question like this and answer it by looking at past setups.

25. If F is the foreman of the student jury, which one of the following is among the people who must also be on the student jury?

    (A) B
    (B) C
    (C) E
    (D) M
    (E) O

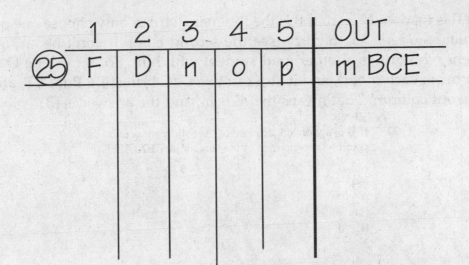

	1	2	3	4	5	OUT
㉕	F	D	n	o	p	m BCE

First of all, there's an FM antiblock, so if F is in, M is out (eliminate (D)). And, there's a DF block, so D is in. Now, if F is the foreman, there can only be two members of the jury that are graduate students (the second clue dictates that). So, all other graduates go in the out column, which means you can eliminate (A), (B), and (C). That leaves us with (E), which you can either get by eliminating everything else, or completing the diagram with everyone who is left (N, O, and P).

26. If B is the foreman of the student jury, which one of the following is among the people who must also be on the student jury?

(A) C
(B) E
(C) M
(D) O
(E) P

	1	2	3	4	5	OUT
㉕	F	D	n	o	p	m BCE
㉖	B	n	E			DFC

If B is in, then N is in. If B is the foreman, we can only choose one other graduate student for the jury (see the second clue). It can't be any grad student who brings another grad student with him. So, it can't be D or F (they bring each other), and it also can't be C (C brings E). Put D, F, and C in the out column. That means that E is in, and the answer is (B).

27. If B is appointed, any one of the following people could be the foreman of the student jury EXCEPT

   (A) C
   (B) E
   (C) M
   (D) N
   (E) P

If B is in, then N is in. Since this is an EXCEPT question, you can eliminate (D). Now, think about how we answered the last question, and check out the answers. (A) is asking us if C could be the foreman if B is on the jury. If C is the foreman, we can only choose one other graduate student for the jury (see the second clue). It can't be any grad student who brings another grad student with him. But C brings E, so we'd have B, E, and C, which is no good if C is the foreman. So, the answer is (A). (Don't forget to cross out scenarios that don't work.)

28. If neither B nor E is appointed to the student jury, which one of the following can be true?

   (A) C is appointed.
   (B) M is appointed.
   (C) D is the foreman.
   (D) N is the foreman.
   (E) P is the foreman.

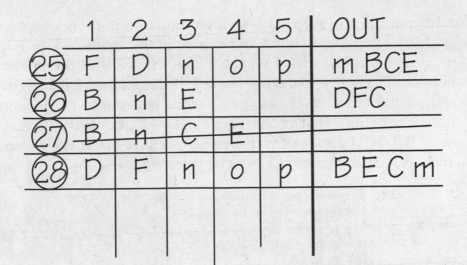

	1	2	3	4	5	OUT
25	F	D	n	o	p	m BCE
26	B	n	E			DFC
27	~~B~~	~~n~~	~~C~~	~~E~~		
28	D	F	n	o	p	BECm

Put B and E in the "out column." If E is out, then C must be out (that's the contrapositive of "if C then E"). That eliminates (A). The remaining grad students, D and F, go in, and F's presence means M is out, which eliminates (B). Since D and F are the only possible grad students who can be appointed, either D or F is the foreman (the foreman must be an member belonging to the group from which exactly two members are appointed). So, (C) can be true.

29. If the foreman of the student jury is to be an undergraduate student, which one of the following must be true?

   (A) If C is appointed, N is also appointed.
   (B) If C is appointed, O is also appointed.
   (C) If D is appointed, B is also appointed.
   (D) If D is appointed, N is also appointed.
   (E) If D is appointed, O is also appointed.

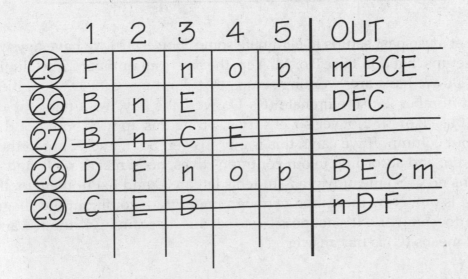

	1	2	3	4	5	OUT
25	F	D	n	o	p	m BCE
26	B	n	E			DFC
27	~~B~~	~~n~~	~~C~~	~~E~~		
28	D	F	n	o	p	BECm
29	~~C~~	~~E~~	~~B~~			~~nDF~~

The foreman is an undergrad, so there must be two undergrads and three grads in. Keep that in mind and check out the answers. For (A), let's see if it's true that if C is in, N must be in. Let's put C in and put N out. If that's not possible, we've found our answer. If C is in, then E is in. We need another grad student, and it has to be someone who doesn't bring another grad student with him. That means it can't be D or F (they bring each other). That leaves B. What happens if you have B? You have N. So, there's no way not to have N, which means (A) must be true.

30. The student jury must include at least one member from which one of the following pairs?

    (A) B, M
    (B) C, D
    (C) E, N
    (D) F, M
    (E) O, P

Let's use past setups to eliminate some choices. Do we have any working setups that don't use B or M? Yep, the one from number 25, so eliminate (A). Do we have any working setups that don't use C or D? Yep, the one from number 26, so eliminate (B). Do we have any working setups that don't use E or N? Not yet, so let's try it setting this up with both E and N in the out column. If we can't, this is our answer. So, E and N are in the out column, and according to our contrapositives, no N means no B, and no E means no C. So the only grad students left are D and F. Put them in. If F is in, M is out. Now there aren't enough undergrads to fill out our diagram. This doesn't work. It's not possible to set this diagram up without E and N. That means (C) is our answer.

Example 6

Four cities—Boston, Chicago, Los Angeles, and New York—are to be visited for a promotional tour of a new weight-loss program. There are six stops on the tour. On each stop exactly one of the cities is visited, and cities can be visited more than once. The schedule of the visits must meet the following conditions:

Each city is visited at least once.

No city is visited twice in a row.

Boston is not visited first.

New York is visited third or sixth or both, and it may also be visited on other days.

If Chicago is visited first, then New York is not visited sixth.

Here's the diagram:

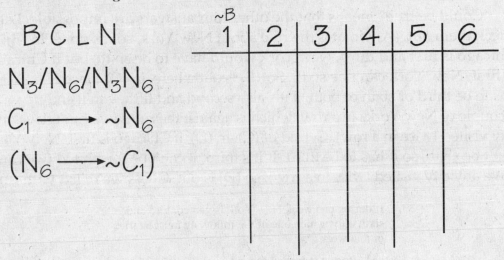

$$B\ C\ L\ N$$
$$N_3/N_6/N_3N_6$$
$$C_1 \longrightarrow \sim N_6$$
$$(N_6 \longrightarrow \sim C_1)$$

TYPE: Assignment

We know that B can't be first, so put up that restriction. And don't forget that contrapositive! Note that we can't put that New York stuff on the diagram, because New York can be places other than 3 and 6.

31. Which one of the following could be the schedule of the visits for one week, for the days of first through sixth, respectively?

(A) Chicago, Boston, New York, Los Angeles, Chicago, Chicago

(B) Chicago, Boston, New York, Los Angeles, Boston, New York

(C) Los Angeles, Boston, Chicago, New York, Los Angeles, Boston

(D) Los Angeles, Chicago, New York, Boston, Los Angeles, Boston

(E) Los Angeles, Chicago, New York, Los Angeles, New York, Chicago

Check your clues and systematically eliminate choices. Each city has to be visited at least once, which eliminates (E) (no Boston). We can't have any city visited twice in a row, which eliminates (A) (Chicago Chicago). New York has to be third or sixth or both, so eliminate (C). If Chicago is first, New York can't be sixth, so eliminate (B). What's left? (D), which is the answer.

32. Which one of the following could be true of one week's schedule of visits?

(A) Boston is visited both third and sixth.
(B) Chicago is visited both first and third.
(C) New York is visited both second and fifth.
(D) Chicago is visited first and New York is visited fourth.
(E) New York is visited third and Chicago is visited sixth.

"Could be true" means that the other four answers are impossible. Let's check them out. (A) violates the rule about New York, so it's gone. In (B), if Chicago is first and third, New York would have to be sixth, but if Chicago is first, New York can't be sixth. So, (B) is outta here. In (C), since New York has to be third or sixth or both, if it's also second and fifth, you'll end up with a couple of New Yorks in a row, which is against the rules (we can't have any city visited twice in a row). Get rid of (C). In (D), if Chicago is first, New York can't be sixth, so it has to be third. If it's third, it can't be fourth too (we can't have any city visited twice in a row), so (D) is out. Guess we're left with (E).

33. If during one week New York is visited third and sixth only, which one of the following must be true of that week?

(A) Boston is visited second.
(B) Chicago is visited fifth.
(C) Los Angeles is visited first.
(D) Boston is visited exactly two times.
(E) Los Angeles is visited exactly two times.

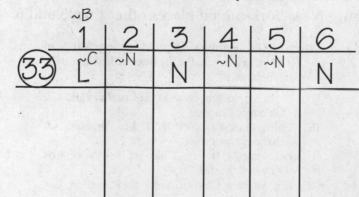

Go to your most restricted place. First. Boston can't be there. Check out the contrapositive of the last clue: if New York is sixth, Chicago isn't first. We also know that New York isn't first, because the question says so. Therefore, the only city that can be visited first is Los Angeles. That's (C).

34.   If Chicago is visited first and sixth only, which one of the following must be true?

   (A)   One other city besides Chicago is visited exactly twice.
   (B)   The city that is visited third is not visited fifth.
   (C)   Los Angeles is visited immediately before Boston is visited.
   (D)   Either Boston or Los Angeles is visited fifth.
   (E)   Either Los Angeles or New York is visited second.

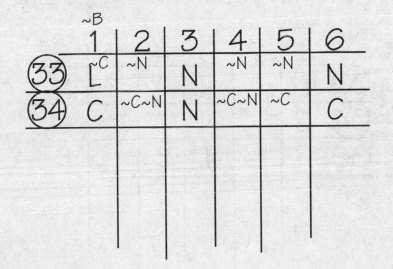

If Chicago is first and sixth, New York must be third. There are three empty spaces left on this diagram, and three cities we can use to fill them: New York, Los Angeles, and Boston. Spaces 2, 4, and 5, respectively, could be LLN, LLB, LBN, BLN, BBN, or BBL. No matter how you fill in those spaces, another city besides Chicago is there more than once. That's (A).

35.   Which one of the following CANNOT be true of one week's schedule of visits?

   (A)   Boston is visited second and Chicago is visited fifth.
   (B)   Chicago is visited first and New York is visited second.
   (C)   Chicago is visited first and New York is visited fifth.
   (D)   Los Angeles is visited first and New York is visited second.
   (E)   Los Angeles is visited second and New York is visited fifth.

That Chicago-New York clue is definitely our best, most restricted clue, so let's start there. (B) and (C) both involve that connection, so let's check those out first. In (B), if Chicago is first, we know that New York isn't sixth. That means it's third. But the rest of (B) says New York is second. We can't have any city visited twice in a row, so (B) cannot be true.

36. If Boston is visited exactly twice but that city is visited neither second nor third, which one of the following could be true?

   (A) One city is visited exactly three times.
   (B) Three cities are visited exactly one time each.
   (C) New York is not visited immediately before Boston is visited.
   (D) Chicago is visited third.
   (E) New York is visited fifth.

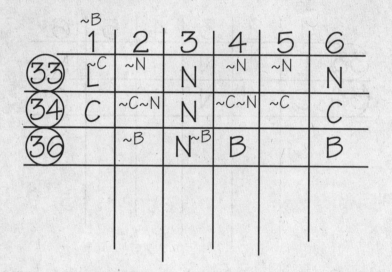

So, Boston can't be first, second, or third. That leaves fourth, fifth, and sixth. It has to be visited twice, and we can't have any city visited twice in a row, so put Boston in fourth and sixth. That forces New York in third. That eliminates (D) and (C). Okay, let's check out the rest of the answers, because "could be true" means the other four are impossible. For (A), can you fill the same city in all the remaining spaces? Nope. We can't have any city visited twice in a row. Eliminate (A). For (B), can you put a different city in each of the remaining spaces? Yes, but how many cities are visited exactly one time each? Two. Eliminate (B). We're left with (E).

Example 7

Nine swimmers—Angus, Bridget, Caleb, Darla, Eugene, Faith, Garth, Hannah, and Ives—are each placed in one of three groups. The three fastest swimmers are placed in the Shark group; the three slowest swimmers are placed in the Guppy group. The remaining three are placed in the Minnow group. Each group has exactly three swimmers.

Darla swims faster than Bridget.
Bridget swims faster than both Eugene and Faith.
Eugene swims faster than Hannah.
Hannah swims faster than Caleb.
Caleb swims faster than Ives.
Faith swims faster than both Angus and Garth.

Here's the diagram:

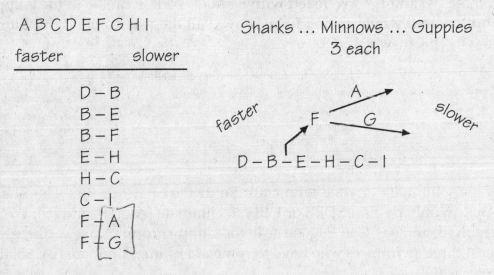

TYPE: Non-Assignment, Range

First, symbolize all the clues SEPARATELY, keeping track of "faster" and "slower." Then, combine all the clues to make the longest chain possible. The good thing about games like this one is that once you draw your diagram, you never really have to touch it again. Just remember to keep track of the Sharks, Minnows and Guppies.

37. How many different combinations of swimmers could form the Shark group?

   (A) 1
   (B) 2
   (C) 3
   (D) 4
   (E) 6

We know that D and B are definitely in the Shark group. The third swimmer in that group is either F or E. So, the Shark group is either DBF or DBE. That's 2, and that's (B).

38. Which one of the following swimmers could be in the Minnow group but cannot be in the Guppy group?

(A) Angus
(B) Bridget
(C) Eugene
(D) Faith
(E) Ives

First, we know that B is in the Shark group, so eliminate (B). Anyone who's too far to the right can be in the Guppy group, like I and A, so eliminate (A) and (E). We're left with E and F. Well, F can be in the Guppy group too; that whole chain can be shoved all the way to the right. Eliminate (D). The answer is (C).

39. Which one of the following swimmers could be placed in any one of the three groups?

(A) Angus
(B) Eugene
(C) Faith
(D) Garth
(E) Ives

First, eliminate anyone who can't be in the Shark group. The Shark group can only be either DBE or DBF, so eliminate (A), (D), and (E). We're left with (B) and (C). Can Eugene be in the Guppy group? No way; there are at least three swimmers who have to come after him. Eliminate (B). So, the answer is (C).

40. The composition of each group can be completely determined if which one of the following pairs of swimmers is known to be in the Minnow group?

(A) Angus and Faith
(B) Angus and Hannah
(C) Caleb and Eugene
(D) Faith and Garth
(E) Garth and Hannah

Since we know that the Shark group can only be DBE or DBF, the positions of E and F would be the key. Eliminate (B) and (E). Next, let's try the rest. In (A), if we know that A and F are in the Minnow group, do we know who the third swimmer in that group is? Could be C, could be G. Eliminate (A). In (C), if we know that C and E are in the Minnow group, we know that the third swimmer in that group must be H. We also know that the Shark group is DBF. That means the Guppy group is AGI. Bingo. The answer is (C).

41. Which one of the following pairs of swimmers cannot be in the same group as Angus?

    (A) Caleb and Ives
    (B) Eugene and Garth
    (C) Faith and Garth
    (D) Eugene and Hannah
    (E) Garth and Hannah

Try them. In (A), can we have ACI? Sure, the other groups can be GHF and DBE. Eliminate (A). In (B), can we have AEG? Sure, the other groups can be DBF and CHI. Eliminate (B). In (C), can we have AFG? Sure, the other groups can be HCI and DBE. Eliminate (C). In (D), can we have AEH? Sure, the other groups can be GCI and DBF. Well, that leaves us with (E). Let's just check to make sure. AGH? Nope. If that's the Minnow group, only C and I are left for the Guppies and DBEF would have to be the Sharks. No good. The answer is (E).

Example 8

Three types of files—contracts, deeds, and wills—are stored in four sealed drawers. For each of the three types of files, there are exactly three drawers that contain that type. Four tags accurately reflecting the contents of the drawers were created. However, only two of the tags were placed on the correct drawers, and the other two tags were placed on the wrong drawers. As a result, the drawers are tagged as follows:

Drawer 1—Contracts and deeds
Drawer 2—Contracts and wills
Drawer 3—Deeds and wills
Drawer 4—Contracts, deeds and wills

Here's the diagram:

CDW

	1	2	3	4
2 tagged wrong				
original	CD	CW	DW	CDW

TYPE: Assignment

Well, all we can do is put in the current setup, and wait and see what we find out from the questions. Knowing that exactly two drawers are incorrectly tagged is going to be a HUGE help.

42. If Drawer 3 actually contains no contracts, which one of the following must be true?

   (A) Drawer 1 is correctly tagged.
   (B) Drawer 2 is correctly tagged.
   (C) Drawer 3 is correctly tagged.
   (D) Drawer 1 contains no contracts.
   (E) Drawer 2 contains no deeds.

	1	2	3	4
original	CD	CW	DW	CDW
42	C	C	DW	C

Sounds like Drawer 3 is tagged correctly. After all, if there are three drawers that contain each type of file, and 3 doesn't have contracts, it must have deeds and wills, which is what its tag says it has. The answer is (C).

43. If Drawer 4 actually contains no contracts, which one of the following must be true?

   (A) Drawer 3 is correctly tagged.
   (B) Drawer 4 is correctly tagged.
   (C) Drawer 1 is incorrectly tagged.
   (D) Drawer 2 is incorrectly tagged.
   (E) Drawer 3 is incorrectly tagged.

	1	2	3	4
original	CD	CW	DW	CDW
42	C	C	DW	C
43	CD	CW	CDW	DW

what about the switch?

Sounds like Drawer 4 is incorrectly tagged. And if it doesn't contain contracts, the other three drawers do. That means Drawer 3 is incorrectly tagged, because its current tag doesn't include contracts. The answer is (E).

44. If Drawer 1 is correctly tagged, which one of the following must be true?

   (A) Drawer 2 contains no contracts.
   (B) Drawer 2 contains no deeds.
   (C) Drawer 2 contains no wills.
   (D) Drawer 4 contains some contracts.
   (E) Drawer 4 contains some wills.

	1	2	3	4
original	CD	CW	DW	CDW
42	C	C	DW	C
43	CD	CW	CDW	DW
44	CD	W	W	W

If Drawer 1 is correctly tagged, then all three other drawers must have wills in them. That's all we really know, so the answer is (E).

45. If Drawer 1 and Drawer 4 are the wrongly tagged drawers, which one the following must be true?

(A) Drawer 1 contains some files of all three types.
(B) Drawer 2 contains some files of all three types.
(C) Drawer 3 contains some files of all three types.
(D) Drawer 3 contains no deeds.
(E) Drawer 3 contains no wills.

	1	2	3	4
original	CD	CW	DW	CDW
42	C	C	DW	C
43	CD	CW	CDW	DW
44	CD	W	W	W
45	CDW	CW	DW	CD

If Drawers 1 and 4 are wrong, they each have each other's tag. So, there are really contracts, deeds, and wills in 1, and contracts and deeds in 4. The answer is (A).

46. If Drawer 1 and Drawer 4 are the correctly tagged drawers, which one the following must be true?

(A) Both Drawer 1 and Drawer 2 contain contracts.
(B) Both Drawer 1 and Drawer 2 contain deeds.
(C) Both Drawer 1 and Drawer 3 contain deeds.
(D) Both Drawer 2 and Drawer 3 contain contracts.
(E) Both Drawer 3 and Drawer 4 contain deeds.

	1	2	3	4
original	CD	CW	DW	CDW
42	C	C	DW	C
43	CD	CW	CDW	DW
44	CD	W	W	W
45	CDW	CW	DW	CD
46	CD	DW	CW	CDW

If 1 and 4 are correct, 2 and 3 must be incorrect, and have each other's tags. That means there are deeds and wills in 2 and contracts and wills in 3. So, the answer is (B).

47. If at least contracts and deeds are known to be in Drawer 4, which one of the following must be true?

(A) If Drawer 1 contains at least contracts and deeds, Drawer 2 contains wills.

(B) If Drawer 1 contains only contracts and deeds, Drawer 2 contains contracts.

(C) If Drawer 2 contains only contracts and deeds, Drawer 1 does not contain contracts.

(D) If Drawer 2 contains at least deeds and wills, Drawer 4 does not contain wills.

(E) If Drawer 3 contains at least contracts and wills, Drawer 2 does not contain wills.

	1	2	3	4
original	CD	CW	DW	CDW
42	C	C	DW	C
43	CD	CW	CDW	DW
44	CD	W	W	W
45	CDW	CW	DW	CD
46	CD	DW	CW	CDW
47	CDW/CD	CW	DW	CD/CDW

The information in the question tells us that 4 either contains only contracts and deeds, or is correctly tagged. Either way, 2 and 3 are correctly tagged. (A) checks out, so that's the answer.

Example 9

An executive is attending her company's annual convention. The convention features speeches, six of which are to be attended by the executive. The executive must attend two speeches from among three speeches from the research department—B, C, and D; two from among four speeches from the advertising department—F, G, H, and J; and two from among three speeches from the marketing department—P, Q, and R. The following restrictions apply:

If the executive attends G, then she must also attend C.

If the executive attends F, then she will attend neither C nor H.

If the executive attends P, then she will attend neither R nor J.

If the executive attends both C and H, then C is attended some time before H.

P cannot be the fifth speech attended by the executive unless one of the speeches from the advertising department is the first speech attended.

Here's the diagram:

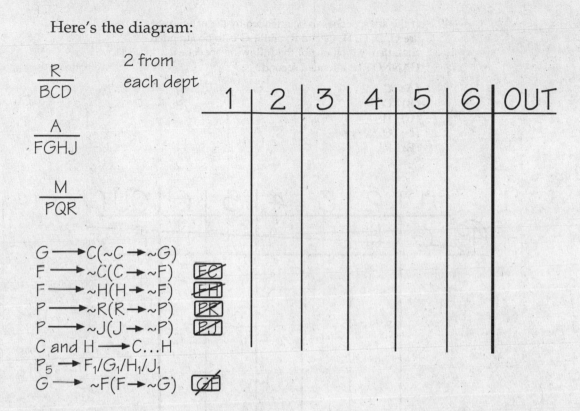

$$\frac{R}{BCD}$$

2 from each dept

$$\frac{A}{FGHJ}$$

$$\frac{M}{PQR}$$

1	2	3	4	5	6	OUT

$G \longrightarrow C(\sim C \longrightarrow \sim G)$

$F \longrightarrow \sim C(C \longrightarrow \sim F)$ ~~FC~~

$F \longrightarrow \sim H(H \longrightarrow \sim F)$ ~~FH~~

$P \longrightarrow \sim R(R \longrightarrow \sim P)$ ~~PR~~

$P \longrightarrow \sim J(J \longrightarrow \sim P)$ ~~PJ~~

C and $H \longrightarrow C...H$

$P_5 \longrightarrow F_1/G_1/H_1/J_1$

$G \longrightarrow \sim F(F \longrightarrow \sim G)$ ~~GF~~

TYPE: Assignment

Contrapositives on parade! Remember, one in and one out is an antiblock (that's how we got the FC, FH, PR, and PJ antiblocks). Don't forget the hidden clue in the setup about choosing two from each department. And don't forget that not every element is being chosen, so you need an "out" column. Are you wondering where that GF antiblock came from? Well, we have "if G then C" and "if C then not F" (the contrapositive of "if F then not C"). We can deduce "if G then not F" which is also a GF antiblock.

48.   Which one of the following is an acceptable sequence of speeches attended by the executive?

	1	2	3	4	5	6
(A)	B	R	F	G	Q	D
(B)	D	C	Q	H	R	G
(C)	D	Q	J	C	R	F
(D)	J	Q	C	B	P	H
(E)	P	G	D	H	C	R

Check your clues and systematically eliminate choices. First, if you have G you have to have C, which eliminates (A). F and C are in an antiblock, which eliminates (C). The PJ antiblock eliminates (D), and the PR antiblock eliminates (E). That leaves us with (B).

49. If the six speeches to be attended by the executive
are C, D, G, H, Q, and R, and if G is to be attended
first, then which one of the following speeches
CANNOT be attended second?

(A) C
(B) D
(C) H
(D) Q
(E) R

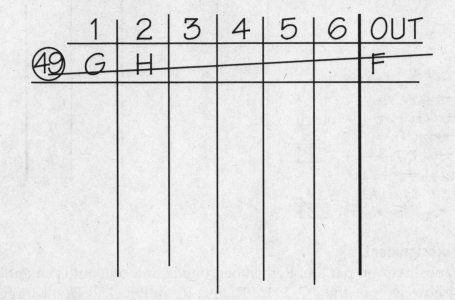

Are any of those speeches restricted? Yes; notice that both C and H are
in. If both C and H are in, C must be before H. G is already first, so now we
look at second. If H is second, that C… H rule is violated. So, the answer is (C).

50. If C, H, and Q are the first three speeches to be
attended, not necessarily in that order, which one of
the following is a speech that CANNOT be attended
fifth?

(A) B
(B) D
(C) G
(D) J
(E) P

Hmm, fifth. What do we know about fifth? We know that P cannot be
the fifth speech attended unless one of the speeches from the advertising
department is the first speech attended. Let's start there. Is either C, H, or Q
from the advertising department? H is. But if H is first we can't have C
(since C…H) and we do have C. So can P be fifth? Nope. The answer is (E).

51. If H is the first speech attended, which one of the following is a speech that must also be attended?

    (A) C
    (B) D
    (C) F
    (D) G
    (E) P

	1	2	3	4	5	6	OUT
49	G	H					F
51	H	J					CGFP

If H is first, C is out (if they're both in, C must come first, which isn't possible if H is first). Eliminate (A). If there's no C, we have to have B and D, because there must be two research speeches. So (B) is the answer. If you didn't see this, remember to keep your pencil moving and eliminate. If there's no C, there's no G (remember your contrapositives!). Eliminate (D). The FH antiblock means that F is out. Eliminate (C). Since we need two speeches from advertising, and F and G are out, J must be in. The JP antiblock means that P is out. Eliminate (E). You're left with (B), which is the answer.

52. Which one of the following is a speech that must be attended?

    (A) C
    (B) D
    (C) H
    (D) Q
    (E) R

Look where you have the most restrictions first. There are only three possible research speeches and three possible marketing speeches, so let's start there. There's an antiblock involving the marketing speeches, so we're zeroing in. If we can't have both P and R, but we have to have two marketing speeches, that means we have to have either P and Q or Q and R. Either way we have to have Q. The answer is (D). This is why it's important to zero in on things using your restrictions.

> 53. Which one of the following is a speech that
> CANNOT be attended if G is attended?
>
> (A) F
> (B) H
> (C) J
> (D) P
> (E) R

Remember that GF antiblock deduction. The answer is (A). In case you weren't clear on how we got it, here's the deal: What happens if G is in? C must be in. And if C is in, F is out (there's an antiblock, remember?).

Example 10

> Six coffees—A, B, C, D, E, and F—are being judged and ranked in terms of taste. The coffees can be ranked, from best to worst, Superior, Very Good, Good, Fair, and Poor, and coffees can have the same rank as each other. Ranks are considered consecutive if they are next to each other; for example, Superior and Very Good are consecutive, and Superior and Good are not. Any coffee that receives the rank of Poor is disqualified.
>
> The ranks of B and E are consecutive.
> The ranks of D and F are consecutive.
> The rank of A is higher than that of C.
> The rank of B is higher than that of E.

Here's the diagram:

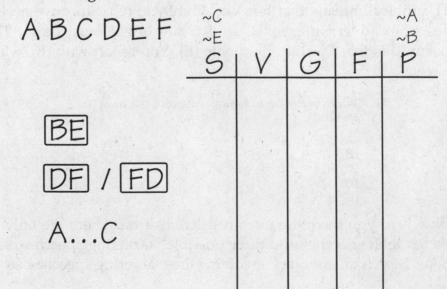

TYPE: Assignment

Wondering why the ranks are on top and not the coffees? Because the ranks have an order to them. Always put what has a natural order on top. The ranks don't change, but the coffees do. Also, the clues are always about the elements, and all the clues are about the coffees, so the coffees must be the elements. Speaking of the clues, if you combine the information in the first clue with the information in the last clue, you end up with that BE block. Use it to deduce that E can never be Superior and B can never be Poor. Also, that A...C info tells us that C can never be Superior and A can never be Poor.

54. If A and D have the same rank, and if F is disqualified, which one of the following must be true?

(A) B is ranked Very Good.
(B) C is ranked Fair.
(C) C is ranked Poor.
(D) E is ranked Very Good.
(E) E is ranked Good.

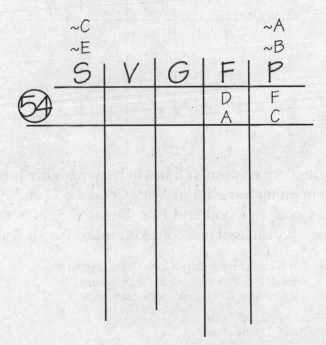

F is disqualified, so put it in the Poor column. That puts D in the Fair column. The question tells us that A and D have the same rank, so A goes in the Fair column. Since the rank of A has to be higher than the rank of C, C must be Poor. That's all we know. The answer is (C).

55. If none of the coffees is disqualified, and B receives a higher rank than either D or F, which one of the following must be true?

(A) Exactly one coffee is ranked Superior.
(B) Exactly one coffee is ranked Very Good.
(C) Exactly two coffees are ranked Very Good.
(D) At least one coffee is ranked Very Good and at least one coffee is ranked Good.
(E) At least one coffee is ranked Good and at least one coffee is ranked Fair.

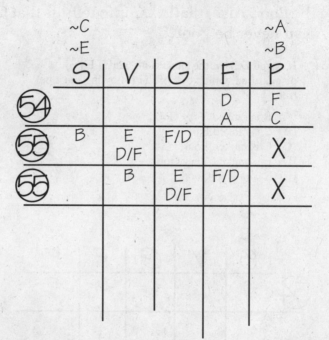

Put an X in the Poor column. If B has to have a higher rank than both D and F, it can be in either Superior or Very Good. So D and F will be either Very Good and Good, or Good and Fair. Either way at least one coffee is ranked Very Good and at least one coffee is ranked Good. The answer is (D).

56. If E ranks higher than A and A ranks higher than either D or F, which one of the following allows all six of the coffees' ranks to be determined?

(A) C ranks Fair.
(B) D ranks Fair.
(C) C and D have the same rank.
(D) C and F have the same rank.
(E) C ranks higher than F.

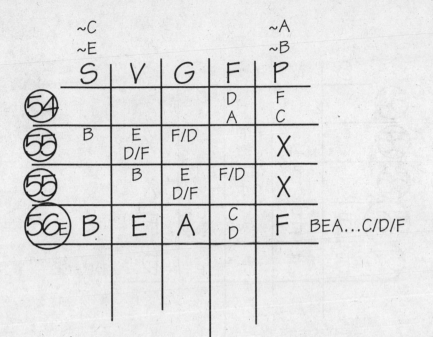

The question has given us this situation: BEA...C/D/F. This guarantees B is superior, E is Very Good, and A is Good. Now, which one of these choices locks the rest of the coffees into place? Try them. In (A), if C is Fair, we still don't know exactly where D and F are. Eliminate it. In (B), if D is Fair, we still don't know where C and F are. Eliminate it. In (C), if C and D have the same rank, that rank still could be either Fair or Poor. Eliminate it. In (D), same problem. But in (E), if C ranks higher than F, C has to be Fair, and F has to be Poor, which means D has to be Fair. That's all the coffees. It's (E).

57. If E ranks higher than A, and C ranks higher than D, exactly how many of the coffees' ranks can be determined?

(A) 2
(B) 3
(C) 4
(D) 5
(E) 6

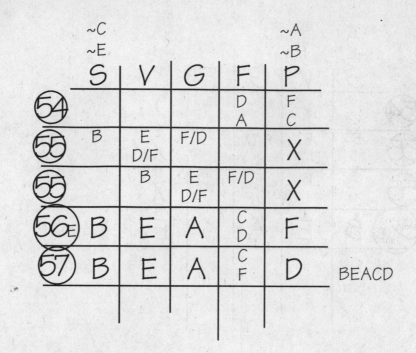

The question creates this situation: BEACD. The only coffee missing is F, which has to be tied with C in Fair, because of the DF/FD block. All six coffees are placed, so the answer is (E).

58. Assume E ranks higher than D and is consecutive with it, and that the ranks of F and E differ. Which one of the following must be true?

   (A) There is a coffee ranked Superior and a coffee ranked Very Good.
   (B) There is a coffee ranked Superior and a coffee ranked Good.
   (C) There is a coffee ranked Very Good and a coffee ranked Fair.
   (D) There is a coffee ranked Very Good and a coffee ranked Poor.
   (E) There is a coffee ranked Fair and a coffee ranked Poor.

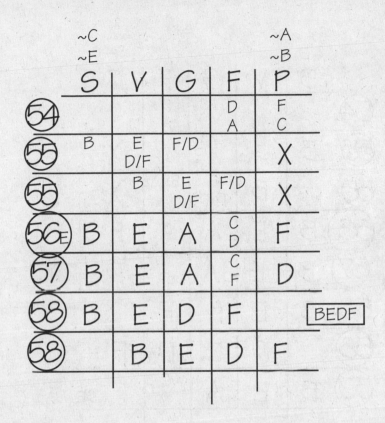

This question created the block BEDF. That's a big block that can either go in Superior, Very Good, Good, and Fair, or Very Good, Good, Fair, and Poor. So, there doesn't have to be a coffee ranked Superior. Eliminate (A) and (B). And there doesn't have to be a coffee ranked Poor. Eliminate (D) and (E). That leaves us with (C).

59. Assume that A ranks lower than E. At least one coffee must have been disqualified if which one of the following is also true?

(A) D ranks lower than A.
(B) D ranks lower than E.
(C) E ranks lower than D.
(D) F ranks lower than A.
(E) F ranks lower than C.

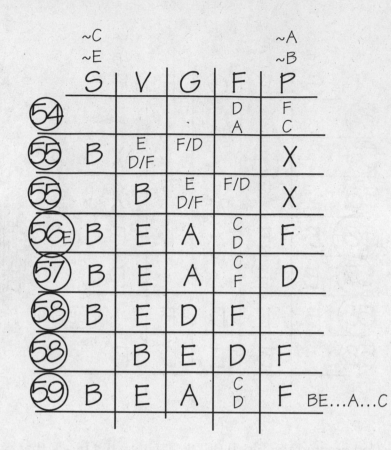

	S	V	G	F	P
	~C ~E				~A ~B
(54)			·	D A	F C
(55)	B	E D/F	F/D		X
(55)		B	E D/F	F/D	X
(56 E)	B	E	A	C D	F
(57)	B	E	A	C F	D
(58)	B	E	D	F	
(58)		B	E	D	F
(59)	B	E	A	C D	F

BE...A...C

This question creates this situation: BE...A...C. We're trying to stretch this thing down to the Poor end, because we want to get a coffee disqualified, so let's see if one of the choices adds something on to the left of B or the right of C. Well, (E) does. If changes the block into BEACF, guaranteeing that at least one coffee is disqualified. That's our answer.

6

ANSWER KEY, LEVEL 3

Example 1
1. D
2. A
3. D

Example 2
4. A
5. B
6. B
7. B
8. D

Example 3
9. B
10. C
11. E
12. A
13. E
14. B

Example 4
15. D
16. D
17. D
18. D
19. B
20. E

Example 5
21. D
22. C
23. E
24. E
25. E
26. D

Example 6
27. C
28. C
29. D
30. E
31. E

Example 7
32. D
33. C
34. B
35. A
36. E
37. E
38. D

Example 8
39. D
40. C
41. E
42. C
43. E

Example 9
44. E
45. B
46. E
47. A
48. E
49. B
50. D

Example 10
51. B
52. A
53. E
54. B
55. D
56. C

EXPLANATIONS, LEVEL 3

Example 1

From exactly seven books—D, E, F, G, H, I, J—exactly four books are being purchased, in accordance with the following conditions:

   If D is purchased, F must also be purchased.
   If E is purchased, G must also be purchased.
   If H and I are both purchased, F cannot be purchased.

Here's the diagram:

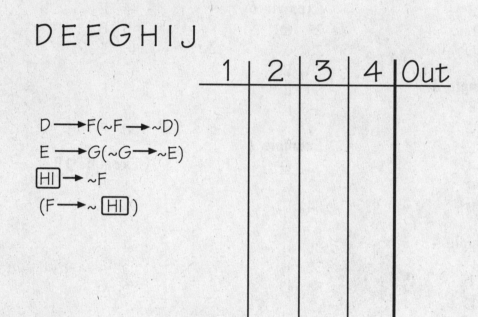

TYPE: Assignment

Not every book gets purchased, so you need the "out" column. Don't forget those contrapositives! And read the questions carefully.

1. If H and I are both purchased, which one of the following must also be purchased?

   (A) D
   (B) E
   (C) F
   (D) G
   (E) J

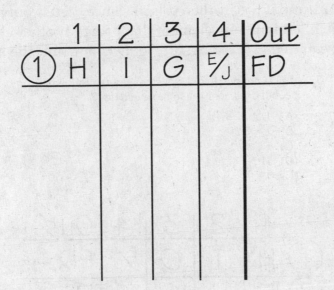

	1	2	3	4	Out
①	H	I	G	E/J	FD

H and I are in, so F is out. If F is out, D is out (eliminate (A)). The possibilities for the other two "in" spaces are either E and G or J and G (E and J isn't possible, because E brings G). Either way, G is in there. The answer is (D).

2. If E and J are both purchased, each of the following could also be purchased EXCEPT

(A) D
(B) F
(C) G
(D) H
(E) I

	1	2	3	4	Out
①	H	I	G	E/J	FD
②	E	J	G		D

E and J are in, and if E is in, then G is in. Since there's only one space left "in," it can't be filled with any element that brings another element with it. That means it can't be D (D brings F). So, D is out, and the answer is (A).

3. If G is not purchased, which one of the following can be, but does not have to be, purchased?

(A) D
(B) E
(C) F
(D) H
(E) J

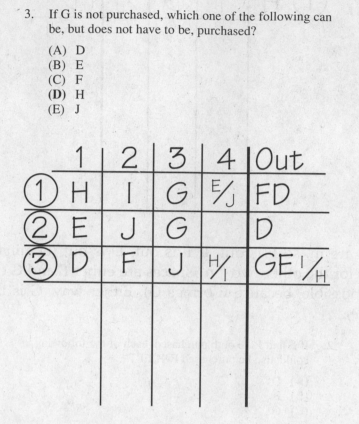

Were you wondering why this game was a Level 3? This question has tricky wording. This is really a weird "could be false" question. First, G is out, which means E is out (eliminate (B)). Now, we have to fill up those four "in" spaces with four of the remaining elements: D, F, H, I, and J. The most restricting clue is that "if HI then no F" situation. So, keeping that in mind, try a few setups. DFJH works. DFJI does too. That's about it. Since D, F, and J MUST be purchased, eliminate (A), (C), and (E). That leaves us with (D). H CAN be, but does not have to be, purchased.

Example 2

A certain music store sells musical recordings only in vinyl, compact disc, and tape formats, and only in folk, jazz, and rock genres. Travis purchases exactly three recordings from the store.

✳ Travis does not purchase two recordings that have the same format and genre.

Travis does not purchase both a vinyl recording and a tape recording.

There are no vinyl folk recordings.

There are no tape rock recordings.

Here's the diagram:

TYPE: Assignment

Don't forget to put asterisks next to clues you didn't symbolize. Notice that we have both horizontal and vertical antiblocks. The big deduction here is that Travis must buy at least one compact disc recording. Why? Well, we have a VT antiblock, and only two each of recordings in the vinyl and tape formats. That forces Travis to buy at least one compact disc.

4. Which one of the following must be false?

   (A) Two of the recordings that Travis purchases are vinyl and two are folk.
   (B) Two of the recordings that Travis purchases are compact disc and two are folk.
   (C) Two of the recordings that Travis purchases are tape and two are folk.
   (D) Two of the recordings that Travis purchases are vinyl, one is jazz, and one is rock.
   (E) Two of the recordings that Travis purchases are compact disc, one is jazz, and one is rock.

Let's try 'em. (A) first: if Travis can only purchase three items, is it possible that two be vinyl and two be folk? Look at the diagram. That situation would force him to buy a vinyl folk recording, which he's not allowed to do. (A) must be false, so that's our answer.

5. If Travis purchases a vinyl rock recording, which one of the following must be false?

   (A) Travis purchases two rock recordings.
   (B) Travis purchases two folk recordings.
   (C) Travis purchases two jazz recordings.
   (D) Travis purchases two vinyl recordings.
   (E) Travis purchases two compact disc recordings.

He's buying something vinyl, so he can't buy any tapes. He has to buy two more recordings, and he has four to choose from: the vinyl jazz, the compact disc folk, the compact disc jazz, and the compact disc rock. Check out the answers. (A) is possible: the vinyl rock and the compact disc rock. Next choice is (B): are there two folk recordings available from that list we just made? Nope. This must be false, so (B) is the answer.

6. If Travis does not purchase a compact disc jazz recording, which one of the following must be true?

(A) Travis purchases either a compact disc folk recording or a vinyl rock recording.
(B) Travis purchases either a compact disc folk recording or a compact disc rock recording.
(C) Travis purchases either a tape folk recording or a vinyl rock recording.
(D) Travis purchases either a tape folk recording or a compact disc folk recording.
(E) Travis purchases either a tape jazz recording or a vinyl jazz recording.

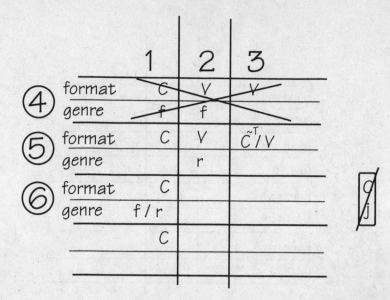

Because we have a vinyl/tape antiblock, we know he always has to buy at least one compact disc. The question rules out the compact disc jazz, so he has to buy either the compact disc folk or the compact disc rock. And that's what (B) says, so (B) is the answer.

7. If Travis purchases exactly one compact disc recording and does not purchase two recordings of the same genre, then he cannot purchase which one of the following?

   (A) a compact disc folk recording
   (B) a compact disc jazz recording
   (C) a compact disc rock recording
   (D) a tape folk recording
   (E) a tape jazz recording

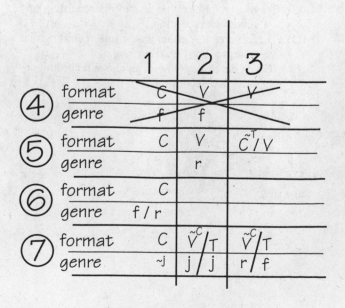

He only gets to buy one compact disc, so the format row is either CVV or CTT. If it's CVV, the Vs have to be jazz and rock. If it's CTT, the Ts have to be jazz and folk. Either way, he's buying a jazz recording, and since the question says he can't purchase two recordings of the same genre, the compact disc he buys can't be jazz. So the answer is (B). Remember, the question says "cannot." Everything else is a possibility.

8. If neither a tape folk recording nor a vinyl rock recording is available, which one of the following must Travis purchase? *give us more antiblocks!*

   (A) a folk recording
   (B) a compact disc jazz recording
   (C) either a tape recording or a vinyl recording
   (D) either a compact disc folk recording or a compact disc rock recording
   (E) either a tape jazz recording or a compact disc rock recording

		1	2	3
④	format	C	V	V
	genre	f	f	
⑤	format	C	V	$\tilde{C}^T$/V
	genre		r	
⑥	format	C		
	genre	f / r		
⑦	format	C	$\tilde{V}^C$/T	$\tilde{V}^C$/T
	genre	~j	j / j	r / f
⑧	format	C	C	V/T
	genre	r / j / f	r / j / f	j / j

Remember, no matter what, he has to buy at least one compact disc recording (otherwise he'd have to buy a tape and a vinyl). Since he now can only buy one possible tape OR one possible vinyl, he'll have to buy two compact disc recordings. That's either CR and CJ, CR and CF, or CJ and CF. Either way, the answer is (D).

Example 3

Each of seven guests at a barbecue chooses one of two types of meals—a hot meal or a cold meal. Each guest is either a child, a man, or a woman. Two of the guests are children, two are men, and three are women. The following is known about the meals the guests choose:

> If the two children and at least one of the women choose the same type of meal as each other, then both men also choose that type of meal.
>
> If the three women choose the same type of meal as each other, then no child chooses that type of meal.
>
> At least two of the guests choose a hot meal, and at least two choose a cold meal at the barbecue.
>
> At least one child chooses a cold meal.

Here's the diagram:

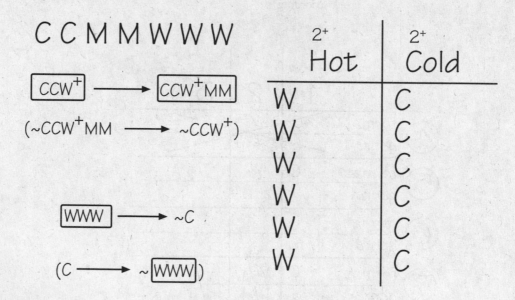

TYPE: Assignment

Those sure are big "if-then" statements! And big contrapositives. Well, there's a big deduction, too, and we can get it from one of those big contrapositives. The contrapositive of the second clue says that where there's a child, there can't be all three women. Well, there's a child in the cold column. So, all three women can't be in that column. So, we know that at least one woman must be in the hot column. Put her in there!

9. If the two men do not choose the same type of meal
as each other, then which one of the following could
be true?

(A) No child and exactly two women choose a hot
meal.

(B) Exactly one child and exactly one woman
choose a hot meal.

(C) Exactly one child and all three women choose a
hot meal.

(D) Exactly two children and exactly one woman
choose a hot meal.

(E) Exactly two children and exactly two women
choose a hot meal.

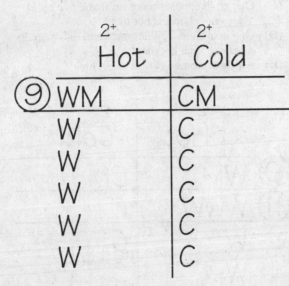

First, put a man in each column. Now, check the answers. "Could be
true" means the other four are impossible. If (A) were true, would any of
the clues be violated? Yes, the first one. Eliminate (A). How about (B)?
Nope, (B) doesn't screw anything up. That's our answer, but since this
game is tricky, let's just look at the others (you wouldn't do this on the test,
of course). If (C) were true, the second clue would be violated. (D) and (E)
each violate the first clue. Yep, it's (B).

10. Which one of the following must be true?

(A) At least one child chooses a hot meal.
(B) At least one woman does not choose a hot meal.
(C) At least one woman chooses a hot meal.
(D) At least one man does not choose a hot meal.
(E) At least one man chooses a hot meal.

Remember our deduction that at least one woman chooses a hot meal?
Let's go over that again: Think about the second clue. If the three women

choose the same type of meal as each other, then no child chooses that type of meal. We already know that at least one child chooses a cold meal. Now, can all three women choose a cold meal? Nope. So, that means at least one woman chooses a hot meal. The answer to this question is (C). If you didn't get that deduction at the beginning of the game, you would have figured it out by cranking through this question.

11. If the three women all choose the same type of meal, which one of the following must be true?

(A) Both men choose a hot meal.
(B) Both men choose a cold meal.
(C) One child chooses a hot meal and one child does not choose a hot meal.
(D) One man chooses a hot meal and one man does not choose a hot meal.
(E) All three women choose a hot meal.

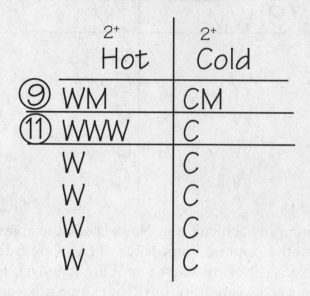

Remember our deduction that at least one woman chooses a hot meal? For this question, if all three women choose the same type of meal, it must be hot, since we know that one woman is already in the hot column. The answer to this question is (E).

12. If exactly two guests choose a cold meal, then which one of the following must be true?

(A) Both men choose a hot meal.
(B) Exactly one child chooses a hot meal.
(C) No child chooses a hot meal.
(D) Exactly two women choose a hot meal.
(E) Exactly three women choose a hot meal.

The second clue will help us here (we can't use the first, because we don't have both children and one woman choosing the same kind of meal). We have to get five people into the hot column. What happens if we put all three women in the hot column? We end up with WWWMM (if all three women choose the same type of meal, no child can, so the other child goes in the cold column). Now let's check the answers. This setup eliminates (B) and (D). Now, let's try changing the cold column to CW. That puts WWMMC in the hot column. Is that okay? Sure, and it eliminates (C) and (E). That leaves us with (A). Notice, in both cases, both men were in the hot column.

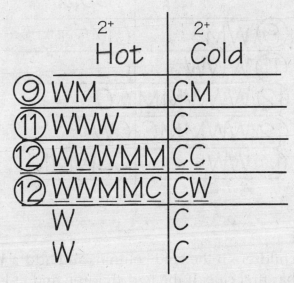

13. Each of the following could be a complete and accurate list of those guests who choose a hot meal at the barbecue EXCEPT

   (A) two women
   (B) one child, one woman
   (C) two men, three women
   (D) one child, two men, two women
   (E) one child, two men, three women

Here comes that second clue again: If the three women choose the same type of meal as each other, then no child chooses that type of meal. Do we have a violation? Yep, in (E). This is an EXCEPT question, so that's our answer.

14. If the two children choose the same type of meal, but the women do not all choose hot meals, then each of the following must be true EXCEPT:

   (A) Both children choose a cold meal.
   (B) Both men choose a hot meal.
   (C) At least one woman does not choose a hot meal.
   (D) Exactly two women choose a hot meal.
   (E) Exactly five of the guests choose a cold meal.

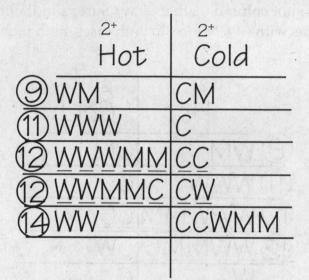

	2^+ Hot	2^+ Cold
⑨	WM	CM
⑪	WWW	C
⑫	WWWMM	CC
⑫	WWMMC	CW
⑭	WW	CCWMM

So, put both children in the cold column, and add a W there as well. Now check out that first clue: If the two children and at least one woman choose the same type of meal as each other, then both men also choose that type of meal. That means you have to put MM in the cold column. Since we must have at least two people in each column, better put that third woman in the hot column. Go to the answers: (A), (C), (D), and (E) all must be true, but (B) is false because both men are in the cold column, not the hot column. (B) is the answer.

Example 4

A game involves ten children, five "throwers" and five "catchers" each on different teams, as follows:

Team	Throwers	Catchers
Red	A	B, C
Yellow	D	E
Purple	F, G, H	J, K

The game is played by pairs of children consisting of one thrower and one catcher of the same color. At most, two pairs can be on the field at a time; the remaining children must be in two rows on the side of the field. The game is bound by the following conditions:

Neither row can include more than four children.

Any two children that are both of the same position and of the same team as each other cannot be in a row together.

Whenever either B or K is on the field, H cannot be on the field.

Here's the diagram:

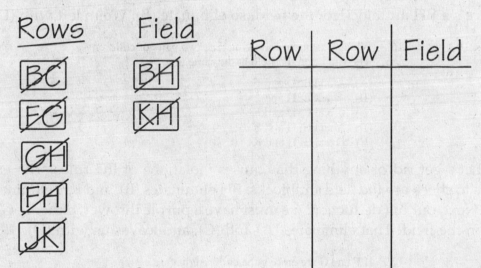

Field= either F, G, or H

TYPE: Assignment

Wondering about all those antiblocks? Well, the "row" antiblocks came from the second clue, which states that any two children who both share the same position and the same team cannot be in a row together. The antiblocks are made up of pairs of children that have the same position and are on the same team. The "field" antiblocks come from the third clue. Now, the big deduction: there must be a purple thrower on the field, meaning either F, G, or H. Why? Because no row can contain FG, GH, or FH. If one purple thrower, say F, is in a row, and another purple thrower, say G, is in a row, the third purple thrower, H, has no choice but to be in the field. So, either F, G, or H must be on the field.

15. Which one of the following is a possible assignment of the children?

	Row	Row	Field
(A)	A, D, E	B, C, H	F, G, J, K
(B)	C, D, F	E, G, K	A, B, H, J
(C)	C, F, H	G, J, K	A, B, D, E
(D)	A, B, D, G	C, E, H, K	F, J
(E)	A, B, D, G, K	C, E, H	F, J, K

Check your clues and systematically eliminate choices. No row can have more than four children, so eliminate (E). Any two children that both share the same position and the same team cannot be in a row together, so eliminate (A) because of B and C, and (C) because of F and H and J and K. There's a BH antiblock for the field, so eliminate (B). We're left with (D).

16. Which one of the following lists two pairs of children who can be on the field at the same time?

(A) A and B; D and E
(B) A and B; H and J
(C) A and C; D and E
(D) A and C; G and K
(E) D and E; H and K

Let's get rid of anything that causes violations of the rules. The easy ones to check are the field antiblocks. BH eliminates (B), and KH eliminates (E). Next, our big deduction: we must have a purple thrower, either F, G, or H, on the field. That eliminates (A) and (C), and leaves us with (D).

17. If F and G are among the children that are assigned to the rows, then it must be true that

(A) A is on the field
(B) C is on the field
(C) E is on the field
(D) B is assigned to one of the rows
(E) J is assigned to one of the rows

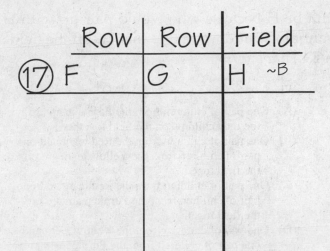

Remember, we have to have either F, G, or H on the field, and according to this question, it's going to be H. Now to the antiblocks. H is on the field, so B can't be. That's (D).

18. If F and J are among the children that are assigned to the rows, which one of the following is a pair of children that must be on the field?

(A) A and B
(B) A and C
(C) D and E
(D) G and K
(E) H and K

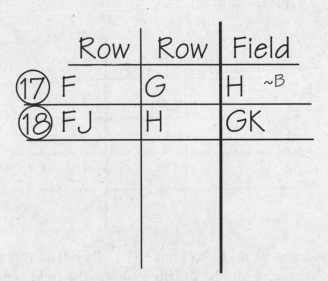

First, let's just eliminate (E), because of the HK antiblock. Now, remember, we have to have either F, G, or H on the field. It's not F, so it's either G or H. But it can't be H because who would pair up with H? It can't be K because of the antiblock, and we're told that J is off the field. So, it has to be G, paired with K. That's (D).

19. Which one of the following CANNOT be true?

(A) One pair of children from the Purple team are the only children on the field together.

(B) One pair of children from the Red team and one pair of children from the Yellow team are on the field together.

(C) One pair of children from the Red team and one pair of children from the Purple team are on the field together.

(D) One pair of children from the Yellow team and one pair of children from the Purple team are on the field together.

(E) Two pairs of children from the Purple team are on the field together.

Let's check 'em out, keeping in mind our big deduction, that we have to have a purple thrower on the field. (A) seems possible. But (B) doesn't have any purple kids on the field. That can't be true, so (B) is the answer.

20. If H is one of the children on the field, it must be true that

(A) A is on the field
(B) D is on the field
(C) C is assigned to a row
(D) E is assigned to a row
(E) G is assigned to a row

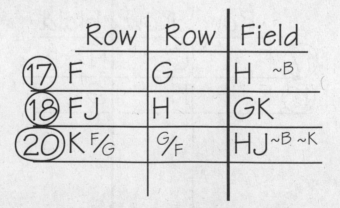

H on the field means no K, so J has to be H's partner. It also means we can't have another pair from the purple team on the field, since there are no more purple catchers. So, F and G go in rows. The answer is (E).

Example 5

Five musicians, and no one else, are competing in a musical competition. The five musicians are ranked from first to fifth, A being the highest rank. The initial order is:

A B C D E
Fiona Gilda Hazel Justine Kendra

In the competition, the musicians will compete in cycles alternating between Red cycles and Yellow cycles, though not necessarily in that order.
In a Red cycle, the following ranked musicians will challenge each other: A vs. B; C vs. D.
In a Yellow cycle, the following ranked musicians will challenge each other: B vs. C; D vs. E.
When two players compete, the winner is awarded the higher of the two positions, and the loser is awarded the lower of the two positions.

Here's the diagram:

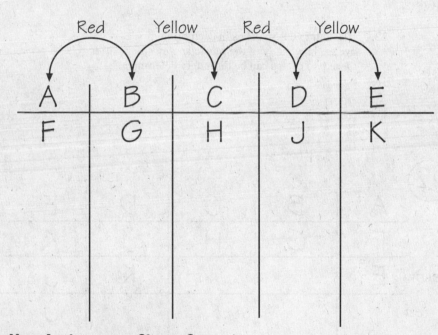

TYPE: Non-Assignment, Simon Says

Nothing to assign here. We just have to follow directions and keep track of the switches. One thing to notice is that during a Red Cycle, the person in the E position doesn't move; she just stays where she is. And, in a Yellow Cycle, the person in the A position doesn't move; she just stays where she is. Also, notice that after only one cycle, it's only possible for a person to move up or down by one rank.

21. Which one of the following could be the musicians' order after one cycle of challenges?

	A	B	C	D	E
(A)	Fiona	Hazel	Kendra	Gilda	Justine
(B)	Gilda	Fiona	Hazel	Kendra	Justine
(C)	Hazel	Fiona	Gilda	Justine	Kendra
(D)	Fiona	Gilda	Justine	Hazel	Kendra
(E)	Fiona	Gilda	Kendra	Justine	Hazel

If only one cycle has taken place, no one could have moved from her original spot more than once. So let's check out the answers and do some eliminating, because in a "could" question, the other four are impossible. In (A), Kendra has moved two spots. That's impossible, so eliminate (A). In (B), both the first person and the last person moved. That's impossible if only one cycle has taken place, because either the first person or the last person always sits out a cycle. Eliminate (B). In (C), Hazel has moved two spots. That's impossible, so eliminate (C). In (D), everything's cool, so that's our answer.

22. If Kendra wins matches in each of the first two cycles, how many of the musicians' positions after these two cycles can be definitely determined?

(A) 0
(B) 1
(C) 2
(D) 3
(E) 5

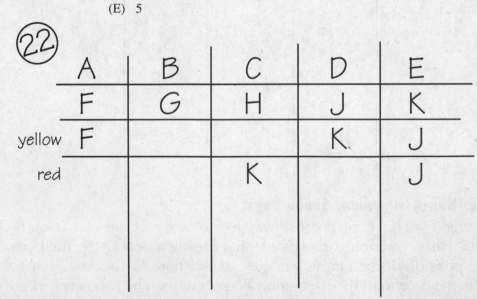

Kendra starts out in the E position. In order for her to be involved in the first cycle, that first cycle must be a Yellow one. So, she wins, and switches places with Justine. Next is the Red cycle, and she wins there, too. Now, she's in the C position. We also know where Justine is: Before the Red cycle, she was last, and during the Red cycle, the last person sits out. So, she's still there, and we know where two people are. That's (C).

23. If Justine wins at least her first challenge, all of the following could be in position C after the second cycle EXCEPT

(A) Fiona
(B) Gilda
(C) Hazel
(D) Justine
(E) Kendra

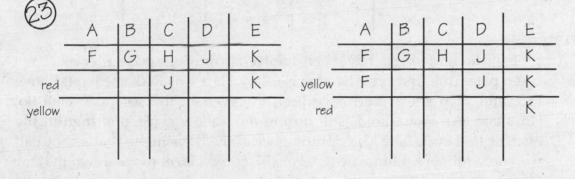

What kind of cycle was the first cycle? We don't know. Let's assume Red is first. Justine wins, so she's in the C position. She could stay there in the next cycle, so eliminate (D). The only other thing we know about that first red cycle is that Kendra sits it out in the E position, so the highest position she could hold after the second cycle is the D position. If the first cycle was Yellow, and Justine wins, she stays in the D position, and Kendra stays in the E position. After another cycle, who couldn't make it to the C position? Kendra. Whatever kind of cycle was first, Kendra was last after it. No way could she move up two spaces after just one (the second) cycle. The answer, then, is (E).

24. If, after the completion of two cycles, Fiona has lost her only challenge, which one of the following could be true?

(A) The first cycle was a Red cycle.
(B) Hazel is ranked lower than both Justine and Kendra.
(C) Fiona is ranked third.
(D) Justine is ranked higher than Fiona.
(E) Hazel is ranked higher than Fiona.

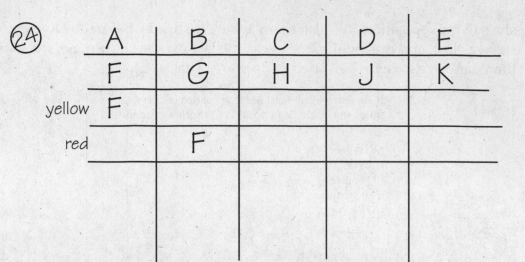

In order for Fiona to have been involved in only one cycle after two have taken place, the first cycle had to be Yellow (if it was Red, she would have lost, and then she would have been involved in the second cycle). So, eliminate (A). Fiona holds still during the Yellow cycle, and then in the next, or Red cycle, she loses, putting her in the B position. That's about all we know for sure. Eliminate (C). For (B), could Hazel move down that far after two cycles if the first one is Yellow? No, because if she loses the Yellow, she stays at position C, and if she loses the next one, she ends up at position D. Eliminate (B). For (D), remember, Fiona ends up in the B position. In order for Justine to be ahead of her, she'd have to be in the A position. Can Justine move up three positions in two cycles? Nope. Eliminate (D). The answer is (E).

25.   Which one of the following must be false?

   (A) Fiona loses challenges in each of the first two
        cycles.
   (B) Gilda wins challenges in each of the first two
        cycles.
   (C) Gilda loses challenges in each of the first two
        cycles.
   (D) Kendra wins challenges in each of the first two
        cycles.
   (E) Kendra loses challenges in each of the first two
        cycles.

Four of these choices are possible; let's check 'em out. (A) is possible if the first cycle is Red. (B) and (C) are possible no matter which cycle is first. (D) is possible if the first cycle is Yellow. But (E) isn't possible, because if the first cycle is Red, Kendra isn't involved, so she can't lose, and if the first cycle is Yellow and she loses, she stays in position E and won't participate in the next (Red) cycle. So, the answer is (E).

26.   If the order after the third cycle is:

A	B	C	D	E
Hazel	Gilda	Kendra	Fiona	Justine

Which one of the following could have been the order at the completion of the first cycle?

	A	B	C	D	E
(A)	Fiona	Kendra	Hazel	Gilda	Justine
(B)	Gilda	Hazel	Fiona	Kendra	Justine
(C)	Hazel	Fiona	Gilda	Justine	Kendra
(D)	Gilda	Fiona	Hazel	Justine	Kendra
(E)	Fiona	Gilda	Kendra	Justine	Hazel

Actually, it doesn't really matter how it looks after the third cycle. What they really want to know is, "Which one of these is possible after one cycle?" In (A), Kendra has moved up too far for one cycle. Eliminate it. In (B), both end people have moved, which isn't possible after just one cycle. Eliminate it. In (C), Hazel has moved up too far for one cycle. Eliminate it. In (D), everything's cool, so (D) is our answer.

Example 6

A certain board game involves six pieces—U, V, W, X, Y, and Z. They are initially set up on the board as follows:

Row 1:	U	V	W
Row 2:	X	Y	Z

The game involves the pieces switching positions. The four possible switches—two of them turns and two of them moves—are described below. No other pieces besides the pieces referred to in the descriptions of the switches below ever change positions.

Turns:

There is a purple turn (PT), in which U switches to the place formerly occupied by V; V switches to the place formerly occupied by W; and W switches to the place formerly occupied by U.

There is an orange turn (OT), in which each U and W switch to the places formerly occupied by the other.

Moves:

There is a blue move (BM), in which the pieces in Row 2 switch places so as to be opposite those pieces in Row 1 that they faced at the beginning of the game.

There is a gray move (GM), in which the pieces in Row 1 switch so as to be opposite those pieces in Row 2 that they faced at the beginning of the game.

Two consecutive turns cannot be followed by a third turn.

If, during the game, the pieces end up in their original positions, the next switch cannot be a move.

Here's the diagram:

U V W

X Y Z

TYPE: Non-Assignment, Simon Says

Things are moving and switching, and there's nothing to assign. We just wait for directions and follow them.

27. If the first switch in the game is OT, followed by BM, which one of the following represents the positions of the pieces after those two switches?

(A) U V W
     X Y Z
(B) V U W
     X Y Z
(C) W V U
     Z Y X
(D) U W V
     X Y Z
(E) W U V
     X Y Z

⟨27⟩   U V W
      ─────────────
   OT W V U

First do OT, which switches U and W and gives us WVU. That already eliminates (A), (B), (D), and (E). Why? Because the next move, according to the question, is the BM, which doesn't affect the position of any piece in Row 1. We're done. The answer is (C).

28. If the pieces' positions are: V U W
                                   Y X Z

which one of the following sequences of pieces in Row 1 is possible after exactly one other switch?

(A) U V W
(B) V U W
(C) V W U
(D) W U V
(E) W V U

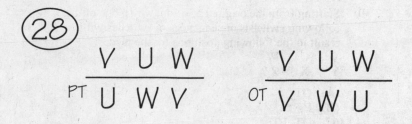

(28)

Try the turns. If we're starting with VUW, and we do the PT, we end up with UWV. Is that a choice? Nope. Start again with the OT. If we're starting with VUW, and we do the OT, we end up with VWU. Is that a choice? Yes, it's (C). That's our answer.

29. If the game started with the pieces in their original positions, and the pieces have switched exactly two times, both of them turns, which one of the following could be the resulting positions of the pieces?

(A) W U V
    X Y Z
(B) U W V
    X Z Y
(C) W V U
    X Z Y
(D) U W V
    X Y Z
(E) W V U
    Z Y X

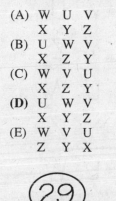

(29)

First of all, we're only dealing with turns, so Row 2 remains unaffected as XYZ. Eliminate any choice that doesn't have Row 2 as XYZ. That gets rid of (B), (C), and (E). We're down to (A) and (D). Let's try (A); in other words, let's try to get UVW to become WUV in two turns. First, the PT changes UVW into WUV. Fine, but that's only one turn. The question specifies two turns. (A) can't be the answer, so it must be (D). (If you really want to know, for (D), the PT changes UVW into WUV, and then the OT changes WUV into UWV.)

30. Starting from the original position, which one of the
following switches or sequences of switches will
result in the following positions for the pieces:

V   U   W
Y   X   Z?

(A) OT
(B) PT
(C) OT, PT
(D) PT, BM
(E) OT, PT, BM

30

	U	V	W
	X	Y	Z

OT

	W	V	U
	X	Y	Z

PT

	V	U	W
	X	Y	Z

BM

	V	U	W
	Y	X	Z

First, notice that the pieces in Row 2 have changed from the original
positions. The only way that can happen is with a BM. Eliminate any choice
that doesn't contain a BM. So, (A), (B), and (C) are gone. Now we're down
to (D) and (E). For (D), can we get Row 1 to change from UVW to VUW by
just using the PT? Nope. The PT changes UVW to WUV. Eliminate (D) and
the answer is (E). (If you really must know, the OT changes UVW to WVU,
which the PT changes to VUW. Then the BM moves X to be across from U,
Y to be across from V, and Z to be across from W.)

31. If the game begins with PT followed by BM, which
     one of the following switches or sequences of
     switches will result in the pieces returning to their
     original positions?

     (A) OT
     (B) PT
     (C) PT, PT
     (D) OT, BM
     (E) PT, PT, BM

(31)

$$U \quad V \quad W$$
$$X \quad Y \quad Z$$
$$\overline{}$$
PT $\quad W \quad U \quad V$
$$X \quad Y \quad Z$$
$$\overline{}$$
BM $\quad W \quad U \quad V$
$$Z \quad X \quad Y$$
$$\overline{}$$
PT $\quad V \quad W \quad U$
$$Z \quad X \quad Y$$
$$\overline{}$$
PT $\quad U \quad V \quad W$
$$Z \quad X \quad Y$$
$$\overline{}$$
BM $\quad U \quad V \quad W$
$$X \quad Y \quad Z$$

First, follow the directions of the question. The PT changes UVW to
WUV. The BM changes XYZ to ZXY. Now, in order to get everyone back to
their original positions, we should first realize that since Row 2 moved, and
needs to move again, the only way that happens is with a BM. Eliminate
any choice that doesn't not contain a BM. That takes care of (A), (B), and (C).
Now the question is, for (D), is the OT enough to get the pieces in Row 1
back to their original places? Let's see. The OT changes WUV to UWV.
That's not the original lineup, so (D) is out. The answer is (E). (If you must

know, the PT changes WUV to VWU, the next PT changes VWU to UVW, and the BM lines up Row 2.)

Example 7

Rick, an artist, uses four special paint colors—yellow, magenta, cyan, and black—that he keeps, respectively, in exactly four buckets—P, Q, R, and S. Each bucket originally contains one color, and Rick is mixing these paints together. A "mix" consists of mixing exactly two of these paints together by completely emptying the contents of one of the buckets into another of the buckets. The following restrictions apply:

   The product of a mix cannot be used in further mixes.
   Mixing the contents of P and Q produces a yellow paint.
   Mixing the contents of Q and R produces a black paint.
   Mixing the contents of R with the contents of either P or
   S produces a magenta paint.
   Mixing the contents of S with the contents of either P or
   Q produces a cyan paint.

Here's the diagram:

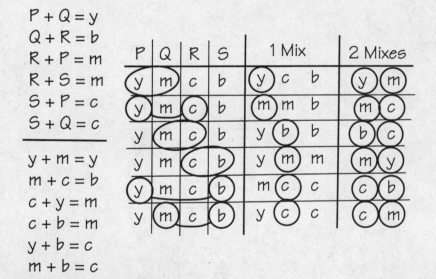

$$P + Q = y$$
$$Q + R = b$$
$$R + P = m$$
$$R + S = m$$
$$S + P = c$$
$$S + Q = c$$
_____
$$y + m = y$$
$$m + c = b$$
$$c + y = m$$
$$c + b = m$$
$$y + b = c$$
$$m + b = c$$

TYPE: Non-Assignment, Simon Says

Whew! Sometimes these Simon Says Games require a lot of figuring out before you even start the questions. First, list the mixes. Then, to make it easier, rewrite the mixes with the colors in the buckets instead of the buckets themselves. If you glance at the questions, you'll notice the questions ask about one mix or two mixes. Make a chart showing the results of one mix of every type, and then two mixes of every type (in the left column, the paints being mixed are circled. In the other columns, the result of a mix, since it can't ever be mixed again, is circled). Yes, it's a lot of work, but that's why this game is hard.

> 32. If Rick creates exactly one mix, which one of the following could be the colors of the paints in the resulting three buckets?
>
> (A) magenta, magenta, cyan
> (B) magenta, black, black
> (C) magenta, black, yellow
> **(D)** cyan, cyan, yellow
> (E) cyan, black, black

Just go to our handy chart and look at the "one mix" column. The only one of these answer choices that's on that chart is CCY. That's (D).

> 33. If Rick creates exactly two mixes, which one of the following could be the colors of the paints in the resulting two buckets?
>
> (A) magenta, magenta
> (B) magenta, black
> **(C)** magenta, yellow
> (D) cyan, yellow
> (E) black, black

Just go to our handy chart and look at the "two mix" column. The only one of these answer choices that's on that chart is MY. That's (C).

> 34. If Rick creates exactly one mix and none of the resulting three buckets contains a yellow paint, which one of the following could be the colors of the paints in the three buckets?
>
> (A) magenta, magenta, cyan
> **(B)** magenta, cyan, cyan
> (C) magenta, cyan, black
> (D) magenta, black, black
> (E) cyan, cyan, black

Just go to our handy chart and look at the "one mix" column. The "no yellow" possibilities are MMB, and MCC. MMB isn't a choice here, but MCC is. That's (B).

> 35. If Rick creates exactly one mix and exactly one of the resulting three buckets contains a magenta paint, which of the following colors could be in the other two buckets?
>
> **(A)** both cyan
> (B) both black
> (C) both yellow
> (D) one cyan and one yellow
> (E) one black and one yellow

Just go to our handy chart and look at the "one mix" column. The "one magenta" possibility is MCC, so the other two buckets are both cyan. That's (A).

36. If Rick creates exactly two mixes and after the first mix exactly one of the resulting three buckets contains a black paint, then in the second mix Rick could mix together the contents of buckets

(A) P and Q
(B) P and R
(C) P and S
(D) Q and R
(E) R and S

Just go to our handy chart and look at the "one mix" column. The "one black" possibilities are YCB and MMB. Let's deal with MMB first. We get that by mixing P and R. That means for the second mixing, we can only mix Q and S. That's not a choice, so let's try YCB. We get that by mixing P and Q. This means that for the second mixing, we can only mix R and S. That's (E).

37. If Rick creates exactly one mix and none of the resulting three buckets contains a black paint, then Rick must have mixed the contents of

(A) bucket P with bucket Q
(B) bucket P with bucket S
(C) bucket Q with bucket S
(D) bucket Q with one of the other buckets
(E) bucket S with one of the other buckets

Just go to our handy chart and look at the "one mix" column. The "no black" possibilities are MMY (which we get by mixing R and S), MCC (which we get by mixing P and S), and YCC (which we get by mixing Q and S). What do all these mixes have in common? They all involve S. The answer is (E).

38. If Rick creates exactly two mixes and exactly one of the resulting two buckets contains a black paint, then it must be true that the contents of the other resulting bucket is

(A) obtained by mixing buckets P and Q
(B) obtained by mixing buckets Q and S
(C) magenta
(D) cyan
(E) yellow

Just go to our handy chart and look at the "two mix" column. The only "one black" possibilities are BC and BC. Notice a trend? Both have C. The answer is (D).

Example 8

A vintner makes six wines. M, N, and P are reds. X, Y, and Z are whites.

* The vintner always bottles and labels the reds first.
* Within their respective groups, the vintner bottles those wines that she makes comparatively more of before she bottles those wines that she makes comparatively fewer of.
* The vintner labels her wines, in their respective groups, in the opposite order of their bottling.

She bottles more of P than of X, and there is no wine that she bottles both more than X and less than P.

She bottles more of Y than of N, and there is no wine that she bottles both less than Y and more than N.

She bottles the same amount of Z as she does of M.

Here's the diagram:

TYPE: Assignment

Okay, these blocks are tricky. They represent correspondence within groups. In other words, if we were to find out that M is bottled first, that would mean that Z is bottled fourth, which is first in its group, the whites. If we were to find out that P is bottled second, that would mean that X is bottled fifth, which is second in its respective group, the whites. Don't forget to put asterisks next to clues you didn't symbolize.

39. If M is bottled first and P third, which one of the following must be true?

(A) Z is bottled fifth.
(B) Z is bottled last.
(C) X is bottled fifth.
(D) X is bottled last.
(E) Y is bottled fourth.

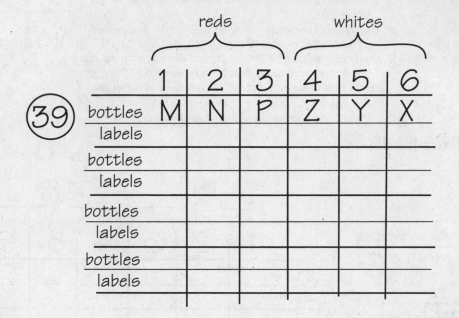

So, the "bottled" row starts with MNP, and the "labeled" row ends in PNM. Since M and Z have "correspondence," Z is fourth in the "bottled" row. For the same reason, Y goes in fifth, and X goes in sixth, or last. The answer is (D).

40. If P is labeled first, which one of the following could NOT be possible?

(A) M is bottled before P.
(B) N is bottled before M.
(C) X is bottled before Z.
(D) Y is bottled after Z.
(E) Z is bottled before X.

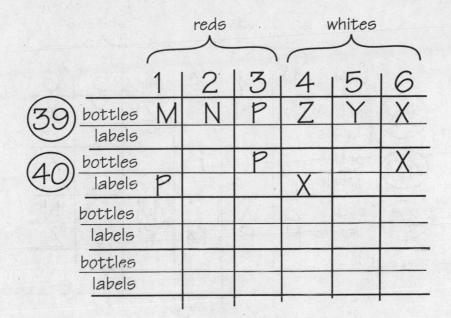

If P is labeled first, it must be bottled last in the red group, or third. Since X has "correspondence" with it, X is bottled third in the white group, or sixth. That's all we know for sure. We don't know the exact relationship between M and N (eliminate (B)), but we know that M must be bottled first or second (eliminate (A)). We don't know the exact relationship between Y and Z (eliminate (D)), but we know that Z must be bottled fourth or fifth (eliminate (E)). That also means Z is bottled before X, so the answer must be (C).

41. Which one of the following is NOT a possible labeling order?

(A) M, P, N, Z, X, Y
(B) N, M, P, Y, Z, X
(C) N, P, M, Y, X, Z
(D) P, M, N, X, Z, Y
(E) P, N, M, Z, Y, X

Just check the "correspondence." Let's go in order and first check the PX correspondence (just think 1-4, 2-5, and 3-6). It's fine in (A), (B), (C), and (D). But not (E), so that's our answer.

42. Suppose the vintner bottles the reds after the whites on a day she labels Y fourth and P second. The order of bottling must be

(A) X, Y, Z, P, N, M
(B) X, Z, Y, P, M, N
(C) Z, X, Y, M, P, N
(D) Z, Y, X, M, N, P
(E) Y, X, Z, N, P, M

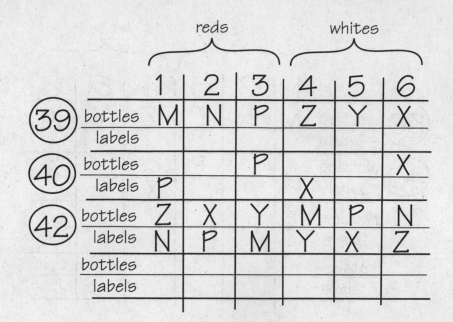

		reds			whites		
		1	2	3	4	5	6
39	bottles	M	N	P	Z	Y	X
	labels						
40	bottles			P			X
	labels	P			X		
42	bottles	Z	X	Y	M	P	N
	labels	N	P	M	Y	X	Z
	bottles						
	labels						

If Y is labeled fourth, it was bottled third—so cross out (A), (D), and (E). If P is labeled second, it was bottled fifth, so cross out (B). All that's left is (C).

43. Suppose the vintner does not label the reds first, but alternates by labeling a white, then a red. If N is bottled first, it would NOT be possible for which pair of wines to be labeled sequentially?

(A) M immediately before X
(B) X immediately before P
(C) P immediately before Z
(D) Y immediately before N
(E) Z immediately before Y

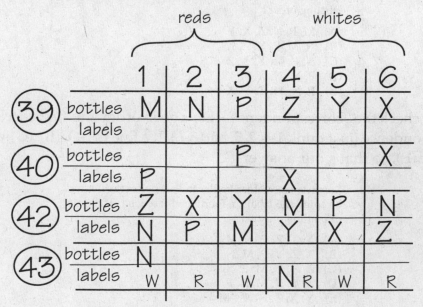

		reds			whites		
		1	2	3	4	5	6
39	bottles	M	N	P	Z	Y	X
	labels						
40	bottles			P			X
	labels	P			X		
42	bottles	Z	X	Y	M	P	N
	labels	N	P	M	Y	X	Z
43	bottles	N					
	labels	W	R	W	N R	W	R

Don't panic. Just follow orders. The order for labeling is now white-red-white-red-white-red. Let's just check the answers for any violation of that new rule. Hey, look at (E). Y and Z are both whites. They can't be next to each other. That's it (remember, the question says NOT). The answer is (E).

Example 9

Exactly six watches—B, C, E, F, H, and J—are being displayed in a row in a jeweler's window. The left-most watch is first, and the right-most watch is sixth. The first, second, third, and fourth watches are all displayed on velvet cushions. The following conditions apply to the display of the watches:

Each watch is either gold or silver, but not both.

Two of the six watches have leather bands and four have metal bands.

Both leather-banded watches, exactly one of which is silver, are displayed on velvet cushions.

Exactly one silver watch is displayed on a velvet cushion.

Watches B and E are displayed to the left of watch F, and watch F is displayed to the left of watches C and H.

Watches B and E are gold.

Watches F and J are silver.

Here's the diagram:

TYPE: Assignment

Okay, which watch do we have the most information about? F. Since F has at least two watches before it and at least two watches after it, it's either in 3 or 4, right? Right, but that's not all we know about F. F is silver, and only one silver watch is displayed on a velvet cushion (so the rest of the velvets are gold). J is also silver, and since we've narrowed down F's position to 3 or 4 (well within the velvet area), J has to be in the non-velvet area, 5 or 6. So, not only are C and H after F, but J is, too. If three watches must come after F, F must be in 3. But wait, there's more. One of the clues says that both leather-banded watches, exactly one of which is silver, are displayed on velvet cushions. That means that the one silver on the velvet cushion, F, is leather. One more thing: Because both leather-banded watches are displayed on velvet cushions, both the fifth and sixth watches (the non-velvets) must be metal. Whew!

44. Which one of the following is a complete and accurate list of the watches that can be gold?

   (A) B, C
   (B) B, E
   (C) B, C, E
   (D) B, E, H
   (E) B, C, E, H

We already know that B and E are gold, so any choice that doesn't include both B and E should be eliminated. That takes care of (A). We don't know how many watches are gold, but we know that F and J aren't. Is there any reason that every watch other than F and J couldn't be gold? Nope. The answer is (E).

45. Which one of the following statements CANNOT be true?

   (A) A gold watch with a leather band is displayed second.
   (B) A silver watch with a leather band is displayed second.
   (C) A silver watch with a leather band is displayed third.
   (D) A gold watch with a metal band is displayed fourth.
   (E) A gold watch with a leather band is displayed fourth.

Remember our big deduction that the third watch is F, which is silver with a leather band. That is the only leather-banded silver watch that is being displayed on a velvet cushion (both leather-banded watches, exactly one of which is silver, are displayed on velvet cushions, and exactly one silver watch is displayed on a velvet cushion). So we know that (B) is false. That's our answer. Anything else is possible, as far as we know.

46. Which one of the following watches must have a metal band?

    (A) watch B
    (B) watch E
    (C) watch F
    (D) watch H
    (E) watch J

Because both leather-banded watches are displayed on velvet cushions we were able to deduce that both the fifth and sixth watches (the non-velvets) were metal. So, any watch that has to be a non-velvet must have a metal band. We figured out that J must be a non-velvet, because it's silver, and only one silver makes it onto a velvet cushion. So, J must have a metal band. That's (E).

47. Which one of the following statements can be false?

    (A) Watch B is displayed to the left of watch E.
    (B) Watch B is displayed to the left of watch H.
    (C) Watch E is displayed to the left of watch J.
    (D) Watch E is displayed to the left of watch H.
    (E) Watch F is displayed to the left of watch J.

We know that B and E are the first two watches, but we don't know which comes first. So, since they can switch places, the answer is (A). This CAN be false. All the other choices must be true.

48. If watch C has a leather band, which one of the following statements can be false?

    (A) Watch B has a metal band.
    (B) Watch E has a metal band.
    (C) Watch C is displayed fourth.
    (D) Watch C is gold.
    (E) Watch H is gold.

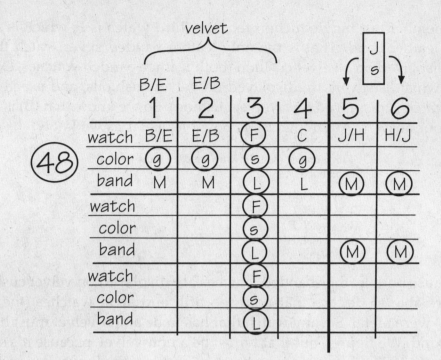

Since we figured out that the fifth and sixth watches (the non-velvets) have metal bands, that means that for this question, C, with its leather band, must be fourth. That takes care of our two leathers. All other watches are metal. Since this is a "can be false" question, that eliminates (A), (B), and (C). We also know that both leather-banded watches, exactly one of which is silver, are displayed on velvet cushions, so if there's another leather-banded watch on velvet (like C in this case), it must be gold. That eliminates (D). That leaves us with (E). Think about this: Do we have any idea whether H is gold or silver? Nope. (E) is our answer.

49. If watch H is displayed fourth, then which one of the following statements must be true?

(A) Watch B has a metal band.
(B) Watch C has a metal band.
(C) Watch H has a metal band.
(D) Watch C is silver.
(E) Watch H is silver.

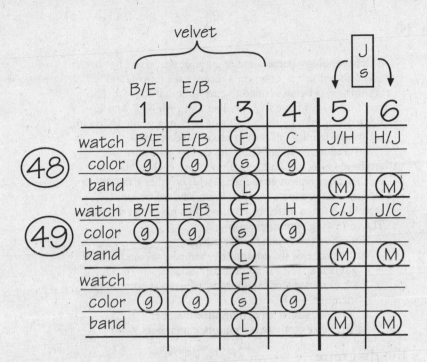

Since we figured out that the fifth and sixth watches (the non-velvets) have metal bands, whoever ends up in those places must have metal bands. With H in fourth, J and C fight it out in those non-velvet places, so both of them must have metal bands. That's (B).

50. Which one of the following statements could be true?

(A) Watch B is not displayed on a velvet cushion.
(B) Watch E is not displayed on a velvet cushion.
(C) Watch F is not displayed on a velvet cushion.
(D) Watch H is displayed on a velvet cushion.
(E) Watch J is displayed on a velvet cushion.

"Could be true" means the other four are impossible. Do you see anything impossible here? Yep. (A), (B), (C), and (E). Just look at the diagram and eliminate them. That leaves us with (D). You could also get this by looking at past setups. Have we ever put H on velvet? Yep. The answer is still (D).

Example 10

The psychology department at a major university has been asked to publish a report on a recent experiment, and a committee is being formed to carry out that request. The committee will have five members—L, M, N, P, and Q. Each committee member holds exactly one of the following positions: faculty advisor, graduate student, or undergraduate student. Only the faculty advisor is not advised. Other committee members are each advised by exactly one committee member, who is either a faculty advisor or a graduate student. Each advised committee member holds a different position than his or her advisor. The following conditions apply:

> There is exactly one faculty advisor.
> At least one of the committee members whom the faculty advisor advises is a graduate student.
> Each graduate student advises at least one committee member.
> L does not advise any committee member.
> M advises exactly two committee members.

Here's the diagram:

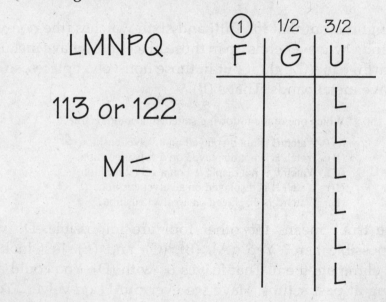

TYPE: Assignment

That first clue is about *how many* of something there is. That's the signal for a distribution tally. We know there's one faculty advisor, so the distribution for the other two columns is either 2-2 or 1-3, making the total distribution possibilities either 1-2-2 or 1-1-3. Why? First, we can't have any zero distributions, because at least one of the committee members whom the faculty advisor advises is a graduate student, and each graduate student advises at least one committee member. Besides, we can deduce that L is an undergrad, because we're told that L doesn't advise anyone, and the only way to not advise anyone is to be an undergrad. Be careful; don't assume that M is the faculty advisor just because she advises two people. She could be a grad student advising two undergrads. This is a tricky game. There are lots of clues hiding in the setup. Read everything carefully.

51. Which one of the following is an acceptable assignment of committee members to the positions?

	Faculty Adviser	Graduate Student	Undergraduate Student
(A)	M	N, P, Q	L
(B)	M	N	L, P, Q
(C)	N	L, M	P, Q
(D)	N, P	M	L, Q
(E)	P	L, M, N, Q	—

Check your clues and eliminate choices that violate those clues. First, there is only one faculty advisor, so eliminate (D). We know that L doesn't advise anyone, so eliminate (C) and (E). Finally, according to our distribution possibilities, 1-2-2, or 1-1-3, (A) and (E) are out. That leaves us with (B), the answer. You might want to draw this possibility on your diagram, just so you have one that you know works.

52. Which one of the following must be true?

(A) There are at most three undergraduate students.
(B) There is exactly one undergraduate student.
(C) There are at least two graduate students.
(D) There are exactly two graduate students.
(E) There are exactly two committee members who advise no one.

The answer choices are about *how many*, so let's use our distributions to answer this one. We figured out that it's either 1-2-2 or 1-1-3. So, the only choice here that must be true is (A).

53. Which one of the following is a pair of committee members who could both be graduate students?

(A) L, N
(B) L, Q
(C) M, P
(D) M, Q
(E) P, Q

First, we know that L is an undergrad, so eliminate (A) and (B). Now, try the others. If M and P are grad students, that means a 1-2-2 distribution.

Those two undergrads would have to be advised by M, but then who does P advise? Remember, there's a clue that says each graduate student advises at least one committee member. So, (C) doesn't work. The same thing will happen in (D): If M and Q are grad students, that means a 1-2-2 distribution. Those two undergrads would have to be advised by M, but then, who does Q advise? (D) is no good, and that leaves us with the answer, (E).

54. Which one of the following could be true?

(A) There is exactly one undergraduate student.
(B) There are exactly two graduate students.
(C) There are exactly two committee members who are not advised.
(D) There are more graduate students than undergraduate students.
(E) The faculty advisor advises all of the other committee members.

The answer choices are about *how many*, so let's check our distributions again. It's either 1-1-3 or 1-2-2. So, (A) is out. But (B) could be true, so that's it.

55. If L is advised by the faculty advisor, which one of the following must be true?

(A) M is the faculty advisor.
(B) N is the faculty advisor.
(C) Q is an undergraduate student.
(D) There is exactly one graduate student.
(E) There are exactly two undergraduate students.

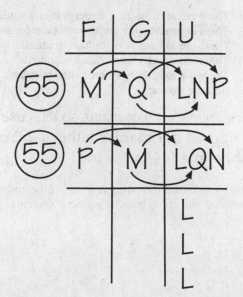

We can't know exactly where anyone is from this question. But here are at least two ways to set it up. Our first setup eliminates (B), (C), and (E), and our second setup eliminates (A), (B), and (E). That leaves us with (D).

56. If P advises exactly two committee members, which one of the following must be true?

    (A) L is advised by P.
    (B) M is a graduate student.
    (C) Q is advised.
    (D) There are exactly two graduate students.
    (E) There are exactly two undergraduate students.

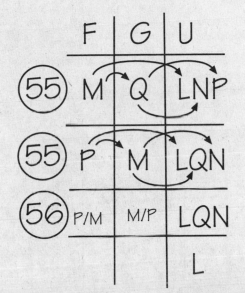

Now both P and M have to advise two people. One has to be the faculty adviser and one has to be a grad student, but we don't know which is which. But we do know that no one else has a shot at being the faculty advisor, so the answer is (C). Wherever Q is, he's not the faculty adviser, which means he must be advised.

ABOUT THE AUTHOR

Karen Lurie has worked for The Princeton Review since
1988, teaching courses, and writing manuals, books, and
software. The following is also known about the author:

    She lives in New York City.

    She was educated by the State of New York.

    She does not hold a J.D., M.A., M.B.A., M.D., M.S., or
      Ph.D.

GRE CAT SCRAP PAPER

THE PRINCETON REVIEW WORLDWIDE

Each year, thousands of students from countries throughout the world prepare for the TOEFL and for U.S. college and graduate school admissions exams. Whether you plan to prepare for your exams in your home country or the United States, The Princeton Review is committed to your success.

INTERNATIONAL LOCATIONS: If you are using our books outside of the United States and have questions or comments, or want to know if our courses are being offered in your area, be sure to contact The Princeton Review office nearest you:

- CANADA (Montreal)   514-499-0870
- HONG KONG   852-517-3016
- JAPAN (Tokyo)   8133-463-1343
- KOREA (Seoul)   82-2-508-0081
- MEXICO (Mexico City)   525-564-9468
- PAKISTAN (Lahore)   92-42-571-2315
- SAUDI ARABIA   413-584-6849 (a U.S. based number)
- SPAIN (Madrid)   341-323-4212
- TAIWAN (Taipei)   886-27511293

U.S. STUDY ABROAD: *Review USA* offers international students many advantages and opportunities. In addition to helping you gain acceptance to the U.S. college or university of your choice, *Review USA* will help you acquire the knowledge and orientation you need to succeed once you get there.

Review USA is unique. It includes supplements to your test-preparation courses and a special series of *AmeriCulture* workshops to prepare you for the academic rigors and student life in the United States. Our workshops are designed to familiarize you with the different U.S. expressions, real-life vocabulary, and cultural challenges you will encounter as a study-abroad student. While studying with us, you'll make new friends and have the opportunity to personally visit college and university campuses to determine which school is right for you.

Whether you are planning to take the TOEFL, SAT, GRE, GMAT, LSAT, MCAT, or USMLE exam, The Princeton Review's test preparation courses, expert instructors, and dedicated International Student Advisors can help you achieve your goals.

For additional information about *Review USA*, admissions requirements, class schedules, F-1 visas, I-20 documentation, and course locations, write to:

The Princeton Review • Review USA
2315 Broadway, New York, NY 10024
Fax: 212/874-0775